W9-AMN-008

SisterStrength

A Collection of Devotions for and from African-American Women

Compiled by
Rev. Dr. Suzan Johnson Cook

THOMAS NELSON PUBLISHERS
Nashville

Published in Nashville, Tennessee, by Thomas Nelson, Inc., Publishers.

ISBN 0-7394-0877-1

Printed in the United States of America.

To Deacon Willie Mae Wright,
a woman who I admire up close; to Deacon Mae Parr-Jones; and to my cousin, Nina, for the many hours of sisterstrength you have given me.

Contents

Part 2
Reflections on My Spiritual Journey

Part 3
The Blessings in My Life

Part 4
Finding Out What Really Matters

Part 5
Tapping into That Spiritual Strength

Part 6
Strength in the Storm

Acknowledgments

I want to first thank my agent and friend, Lois de la Haba, for all her help, encouragement, and strength.

I also want to thank Janet Thoma, Todd Ross, Kathie Johnson, and the rest of the Thomas Nelson team for making this book happen.

God bless you all!

Introduction

For years, I have traveled all over the United States, South America, the Caribbean, and Africa, speaking, representing the executive office of the U.S., preaching, and mentoring. Whenever and wherever I go, the sometimes silent, yet always persistent, plea is the same: "I need strength, my sister." Sometimes words cannot express the need and the plea is simply a look. I get it from everyone I meet, from cabinet secretaries to heads of state. African-American women are very adept at carrying on these conversations with their eyes. We can roll them, raise them up, open them wide, or slant them—we all know the silent meanings.

But sometimes a touch of the hand expresses the need, someone reaching out for my hand, squeezing gently, and asking, "Pray for me, Rev. Sujay." Sometimes I know ahead of time that a sister is up against some mighty forces, and I offer up a quiet but fervent prayer. And still other times, I compile the words of my sisters so that other sisters may find strength from women who have experienced the joys and the pains of life.

SisterStrength is a compilation of devotions for and from African-American women. The devotions are stories of love, success, failure, heartbreak, grief, and hopefully some answers to some of the questions that have been hindering you. The book is written with the hope that you will find strength for the struggles that lay ahead, empowerment for the road you are on right now, and healing for those areas of your life that still hurt you.

My prayer is that by reading this book, your "joy will come in the morning." Today is your "morning," the beginning of the rest of your life. Find strength in the following devotions. Find strength from these sisters and those around you. But most of all, find strength in God.

Part 1

A Word of Encouragement to Sisters

Something Happens When You Say the Name *Jesus*

"Every day with Jesus is sweeter than the day before." I can still hear my mom's sweet voice singing these words in our living room as she gathered all of the children in the nursery for family devotion. My big sister would play the piano, and we would sing hymns. Then Mom would say, "Something happens when you say the name *Jesus*." When she said that, I knew it was time for a great Bible story.

Mom would sit in her big easy chair and all of the children would sit on the floor in front of her. I would sit on the floor with my head resting on her knee as she would tell the stories of the Bible.

As I listened to Mom I could feel that Jesus was not only my savior but my best friend. Mom would tell us that whenever we were scared or confused we should call on the name of Jesus. She told us that because His love was deep enough to die for us, that same love would always comfort and help us in times of trouble.

I have grown up with this truth, and I know it to be so. There have been so many times in my life when all I could say was His sweet name because the sadness and hurt I felt was too great to voice any other word. And I have always experienced peace immediately following the mention of His name, peace that passes understanding. The kind the world knows nothing about. With that peace I am able to go on.

I have passed this practice on to my

daughter, Noelle, who is in college, and she tells me that it brings her that same peace. I now pass it on to you. Something happens when you say the name *Jesus*.

Thought for the Day: *Jesus*

Scripture for the Day: *At the name of Jesus every knee should bow. (Phil. 2:10)*

Marenda Perry, a vocal artist, is a native of Philadelphia, Pennsylvania, and is a scholarship graduate of Combs College of Music and the Curtis Institute of Music (Opera Department) in Philadelphia. After a successful New York recital debut at Alice Tully Hall in the Lincoln Center, she became an artist with the Metropolitan Opera. She was also a soloist for the New York Oratorio Society, the Alvin Ailey/ American Dance Theater, and The National Chorale Council. She has appeared in

Porgy and Bess at Radio City Music Hall and has toured in the production on two continents. Ms. Perry lives in New York City and is a member of Marble Collegiate Church. When she is not touring, she teaches voice privately and introduces opera and chorus to children in the New York City school system.

"I'm Here for You, My Sister"

I press toward the mark for the prize of the high calling of God in Christ Jesus. (Phil. 3:14 KJV)

"Come on, girl, you can do it! Push!" Those are the familiar words a sister hears in the delivery room from the physician, coach, or midwife. The art of midwifery seems to be a lost art today. The term *midwife* means to "whisper in the ear." In essence, the midwife was a coach. The midwife, unlike today's physicians, stayed with the woman in labor and provided continual emotional support, a soothing back rub, and continued instruction throughout labor and delivery.

I can remember the sister in the hospital room next to mine when my first child was born. She was yelling and screaming—"I don't want to push!" My husband looked at me and said, "It's gonna be a long night."

I thank God for the midwives that stood with me in hard times, listening to me, weeping with me, counseling me, correcting me, and most of all praying with me. It doesn't have to be a long night. When trials and testings come, we sometimes hold back and don't want to push with the contractions of life. But you must push, my sister! Press your way to that high calling that Jesus Christ has for your life. I have dedicated my life to being a spiritual midwife and letting sisters know "I'm here for you!" We must recapture the art of "sistercare" by helping sisters birth their destiny.

A Word of Encouragement to Sisters

Thought for the Day: P.U.S.H.—Pray until something happens. As you are pushing, God will perform it.

Scripture for the Day: *I can do all things through Christ who strengthens me. (Phil. 4:13)*

Pastor Jackie L. Green is an ordained minister who serves as the pastor of prayer and pastoral counseling at the First Institutional Baptist Church of Phoenix, Arizona. She is the author of the book *When She Hears the Call*. She serves as a "spiritual midwife" and reformer in the body of Christ in the ministry of prayer mobilization. She is married to Pastor Anthony Green and is the mother of five children.

Good Fridays Always Lead to a Resurrection

Easter 1998 was very special to me as I reflected on some "Good Fridays" in my past. Several years ago I had simultaneous life challenges: As a professional dancer, I was both unemployed and injured. A two-year relationship that I thought was leading to marriage suddenly met a rocky ending. Furthermore, I was angry with God because I felt my prayers had gone unanswered. This unhappy time spawned the worst depression in my life. My self-esteem was abysmal, and I felt small and ashamed.

Looking back, I see that though I felt too low to reach God, God was lovingly involved in my life. In Luke 22:43, Jesus desperately prayed in Gethsemane and God consoled him: "There appeared an angel . . . strengthening him" (KJV). In the same way, God sent angels to strengthen me. The first angel was my dearest sisterfriend, Melody Barnes. Melody was the embodiment of sisterly encouragement. Her encouragement came through words, certainly, but also through listening and simply being there for me. Melody's sisterliness provided an antidote to my sense of loss.

God did not stop there, just as Christianity does not end with Good Friday. God's resurrecting and revitalizing power reached me on Easter Sunday. God sent more angels—Melody's parents, Frances and Charles Barnes. A warm, loving family with an infectious sense of humor, the Barneses came to New York and included me in their Easter celebrations as their "other" daughter. We began the day in worship at Convent Avenue Baptist Church in Harlem and ended with a family dinner.

God nurtured my broken spirit through these angels. That Easter Day with the Barnes family helped spark the beginning of a resurrection in my life.

Thought for the Day: Thank God for a good sisterfriend.

Scripture for the Day:
The Spirit of the Lord GOD is upon Me,
Because the LORD has anointed Me . . .
He has sent Me to heal the brokenhearted.
(Isa. 61:1)

Kimberleigh Jordan is a native of Raleigh, North Carolina. She currently resides in New York City where she serves as an associate minister at Marble Collegiate

Church. Before answering her call to ministry, Kim danced professionally in New York City with the Dance Theatre of Harlem Workshop Ensemble, the Metropolitan Opera, and various choreographers. Her current ministry involves the arts, education, and spiritual development, especially with young adults and women. Her gifts include liturgical dance and worship planning. Kim is a graduate of Union Theological Seminary and the University of North Carolina–Chapel Hill.

The Angel in You

"If we take people as they are, we make them worse. But if we treat them as if they were what they should be, we make them what they can be."

—Johann Wolfgang Von Goethe
Founder, The Hope School

Most children at one time or the other, ask their parents, "Where did I come from?" Well, my mother always responded, "You're God's little angel child. He sent you to take care of us." Somehow that seemed right. So I invented a story about how I put my parents together. I would tell them that I saw them from heaven: Edward, a mannish little boy who sang like an angel in church, was bad as the devil outside, yet always had a good heart; and Delores, a cute little girl with dimples who played the piano and possessed a very proper demeanor, with a tough character and a soft heart.

As my story goes, I decided that they should be my parents. I put them together so that I could come to earth and bring some excitement to their lives. Throughout the fifty years we've been a family, we have brought so much happiness to each other that it seems like a relationship that truly was made in heaven. I told that story so many times that I really began to believe it; or at least I tried to live up to the standard of being an angel. Maybe that's why I believe that there is a little angel in all of us; our God-given, inherent strength.

By accentuating these strengths, our

weaknesses are minimized to a point we can manage them, accept them, or eliminate them. These inherent strengths are unique to each of us. They are what makes *you* uniquely *you*: the way *you* laugh or smile, the way *you* walk, talk or respond to situations. They are *your* tastes in entertainment and food, *your* sense of humor, *your* hobbies, talents, or management style. Anyone who knows you would say that's *your* style.

Sometimes our inherent strengths are overshadowed by others' perceptions and multiple images: the image we have of ourselves; the image others have of us, professionally and/or personally; and the image of the person we would like to become. However, once we can find the common thread in these images and match it to our inherent strength, we can repeatedly leverage it to our advantage. Many of us flounder back and forth between these images, rarely happy with who we are because of what other people think or because of the person we think we should be. And some of us just don't know what our inherent strengths are and how to maximize them.

Here is a quick exercise you can try. List three compliments you receive personally (e.g., friendly, organized, well dressed), three compliments you receive professionally (e.g., smart/skilled, dependable, cooperative), and three attributes you like about yourself (e.g., responsible, professional, caring). Now look at which character qualities consistently show up. Based on the above example, you are a pleasant, smart person who gets along with other people and cares about others, as well as yourself, whether in the workplace or at home. *These strengths are the angel in you.*

When you believe in your inherent strengths and act on your belief by using these strengths, you can more readily identify goals. And once you know what strengths will help you reach those goals, you can then maximize opportunities to achieve those goals. Your accomplishments result in a boost to your self-confidence, your inherent strengths—the angel in you. And the process repeats itself over and over again. I call it the attitude cycle. It affects how we respond to situations, which in turn affects how we respond to others and how well others respond to us.

There are three keys to successfully grow and sustain the angel in you: *Reflect-a-tude, Reflect-a-vision, and Reflect-a-business.*

**Reflect-a-tude*™ helps you keep your self-worth in clear view. And it helps others see the angel in you. Reflect-a-tude

Thinks "I Can"
Thinks Proudly
Thinks Enthusiastically
Thinks Sincerely
Thinks "I Care"

Thinks "Let's"

*Reflect-a-vision™ helps you look beyond the obstacles. It finds the positive in what appears to be negative circumstances. It helps you see the angel in others. Reflect-a-vision

Sees the Potential

Sees the Profitability

Sees Past the Obstacles

Sees the Alternatives

Sees the Ultimate Good

*Reflect-a-business™ helps you keep your commitment to others, whether in personal, professional, or civic relationships. Reflect-a-business

Works to Serve

Works to Improve

Works to Excel

Works to Share

Works to Expedite the Mission

Each of us has everything we need to

live happy, prosperous lives. It isn't necessarily what we do that makes all the difference; it's when and how we do it, influenced by the attitude we reflect to ourselves and the attitude we reflect to others. Our challenge is to exercise our angels—to give them daily strength and never stop looking for the angel in others.

There is a verse that keeps me going when the angel in me is challenged. I give it to you for those inevitable times: "Let us not be weary in well doing: for in due season we shall reap, if we faint not" (Gal. 6:9 KJV).

Come on, angels, let's fly to our highest potential. From one angel child to another, let's enjoy heaven on earth and the treasures it brings! Heaven must be missing a lot of angels 'cause you're here with me right now!

Thought for the Day: Never stop looking for the angel.

Scripture for the Day: *Having then gifts differing according to the grace that is given to us, let us use them. (Rom. 12:6)*

Charlotte VM Ottley has spent eighteen years as an award-winning entrepreneur, ten years as a university instructor, and fourteen years as an award-winning executive producer with CBS- and NBC-owned television stations. She is currently president of C. Ottley Strategies, Ltd., a special market development firm that specializes in developing successful corporate-community partnerships.

The Other Side of Midnight

Webster defines *midnight* as "deep or extended darkness or gloom." Dr. Otis Moss Jr., in his sermon "Learning To Handle Our Midnights," defines midnight as "a bridge between yesterday and tomorrow."[1]

Prepared or not, inevitably each of us will have our midnights. On Sunday, September 21, 1997, at approximately 9:00 A.M. I experienced my midnight. It came like a thief in the night when I least expected it. It came at a time when I thought everything was going well. At that moment a longtime friendship and professional relationship ended. At that moment that unique feeling of trusting, respecting, and supporting, and that special feeling of being trusted, valued, and respected was lost with no hope of ever being regained.

On that day, at that moment, I experienced the deepest darkness and gloom I'd ever experienced. That darkness extended from one day to the next. It was midnight in the morning, midnight in the middle of the day, midnight in the afternoon, and midnight all night. Months later it feels like it happened just yesterday.

In the book of Acts, Paul and Silas prayed in prison at midnight. During your midnight, when your friends betray you and you feel like you have no one to turn to, pray. God is a friend that is closer than a brother. When no words relieve the pain, pray. God is a burden-bearer. There is another side to your midnight.

On the other side of midnight is strength

and power. On the other side of midnight is spiritual growth and a stronger faith. On the other side of midnight, that bridge that connects yesterday with today and tomorrow, God fixes the brokenness in our lives—the broken hearts, broken friendships, and broken relationships.

1. Smith, J. Alfred Sr., Editor. *No Other Help I Know*. (Valley Forge, PA: Judson Press, 1996), 52.

Thought for the Day: Prayer is the greatest healer.

Scripture for the Day:
Weeping may endure for a night,
But joy comes in the morning. (Ps. 30:5)

Marjorie Heidelberg Lawson is a graduate of California State University–Sacramento, with a major in education. For the last seventeen years she has worked as a physical education and movement specialist for the Piedmont Unified School District in Piedmont, California. She is a member of Allen Temple Baptist Church in Oakland, California. She is also President of Breeda Enterprises, a wedding, special events, and meeting planning company. Ms. Lawson has more than ten years of experience in the hospitality industry. She has been featured in *Meeting Monthly's* "Meet the Masters" and *The Crisis* magazine. She has also been recognized by the Oakland Convention and Visitors Authority as the city's "Hometown Hero" and "Outstanding Meeting Planner." Ms. Lawson has been the guest writer for articles on meeting planning for the *Black Convention Magazine.*

In the Company of Exceptional Women

This is the beginning of an incredible journey. What a wonderful opportunity to contribute to a collection of works edited by a friend. How did this shy Bronx woman receive this unbelievable opportunity? Being in the company of exceptional women all my life didn't hurt.

The women who influenced me are unique by any standard. Leading this group is my mother. She possessed a gentle manner that belied her incredible strength. Her children were encouraged to aspire to be the best in their fields. She stressed that we always aim for the gold; the silver or bronze was not an option. She carried herself with grace and dignity at all times.

When my mother died, I felt lost and without hope. Fortunately, I had amassed a wonderful support network. These mentors, role models, sisters, and friends taught me to systematically work toward realizing my dreams. I have tried to make my mother proud by my accomplishments. I tackle everything with an honesty and a tenacity that I learned from her and from these other precious women. Because of their impact on my life, I am confident that I can succeed in all my endeavors.

In the company of exceptional women, I became a sponge, absorbing all that I could from those willing to share their knowledge. I have been privileged to be mentored by a select group of individuals, including an icon in the field of journalism, the widow/partner of a baseball hero embarking on her own literary greatness, a delightful author, and a corporate power broker. This group of exceptional women also included a media wizard, an enterprising inventor, an inspirational and spiritual motivator, an educator, a beautician, and an entrepreneur. These women are my sisters. They have nurtured and guided me in my professional and personal development. They are women of all ages and experiences.

Serving as an apprentice to these powerful women who have distinguished themselves by their vision, mission, and unique legacy, has provided me invaluable training for success. As a result of their empowerment, I have the ability to articulate ideas and interact with all areas of society.

I am exhilarated that I have been able to interact with our country's movers and shakers and its plain folks too. I have stood on a stage with a governor, sat on a dais with the first lady of the United States, had dinner with the mayor of New York City and his gracious wife, in addition to meeting numerous politicians and a plethora of celebrities.

It is a truism that we are what we are because of those who came before us. My exposure to positive role models provided me with the impetus to be a self-sufficient, cultural, spiritual, and effective individual. It's difficult to know what lies ahead in the new millennium, but a strong support mechanism and belief in yourself definitely can prepare you for whatever awaits. The tenacity, strength, and support of exceptional women will provide the confidence to navigate toward the future.

This is certainly the beginning of an exciting time. I am forever indebted to the exceptional women who shaped my destiny and prepared me for the marketplace of tomorrow. My sisters are rare jewels, supporting me, encouraging me, and providing guidance to me in all my endeavors.

Thought for the Day: Thank God for the exceptional women in your life.

Scripture for the Day: *The rib which the LORD God had taken from man He made into a woman. (Gen. 2:22)*

Sonnie Humphrey is a special projects consultant working with a media conglomerate. She is the former executive assistant to the president/CEO and special assistant to the founder of the Jackie Robinson Foundation. She is politically active in the community and serves on numerous boards including the Board of Directors of the New York Coalition of 100 Black Women, the WCBS-TV Advisory Committee for Black History Month Fulfilling the Dream Celebration, the New York

Women's Agenda, and the Zeta Delta Phi Sorority. She earned her bachelor of arts degree from Hunter College.

"If I Have, You Have"

You are my sister, and what you do will have an impact on me and every other sister. If you hurt, I hurt. When you rejoice, I rejoice. As a sister it is my duty to inform the uninformed, because together we control our destiny. Each and every one of us can make a difference no matter what our economic, professional, or social status. All we need is determination and dedication. We have allowed outside forces to keep us institutionalized in hate, deception, greed, jealousy, and destruction. We no longer talk, hug, or help one another as was part of our rich heritage. We have forgotten the old cliché taught to us by our foremothers, "If I have, you have!" This meant that I would help you and be there for you as long as I saw you trying to help yourself, and then you were supposed to pass it on. We are blessed in order to bless someone else. Participating in this book was made possible because a sister gave me an opportunity.

My sisters, we must reclaim our souls and our commitment to one another before it's too late. We have two choices—bad or good. There is no in-between. Believe me, choosing good takes courage, because the grass always looks greener on the other side.

I'm a forty-two-year-old Native Black American woman who lives from paycheck to paycheck trying to make ends meet. I face racism every day. At the end of the day I return to a community that once flourished with family pride but now deteriorates in self-pity. It's time for the self-pity to stop.

I feel good every day I open my eyes because I have a good soul. I feel good about who I am, what I am, where I'm from, and where I'm going. But above all, I love myself.

You must love yourself before you can love others. Stay real, and most importantly don't lie to yourself.

Thought for the Day: Love your sister as you do yourself. But you must first love yourself.

Scripture of the Day: *Old things have passed away; behold, all things have become new. (2 Cor. 5:17)*

Terry B. Williams, formerly of Bennettsville, South Carolina, now resides in Brooklyn, New York, and is a civilian employee of the New York Police Department. She is cofounder of TRADITION, an organization that helps seniors. She is a graduate of Cornell University's Union Women's Study Program and Hunter College, where she received a bachelor's degree in political science. She was an intern with former Congresswoman Shirley Chisholm.

Don't Quit

Often God opens great doors of opportunity for us, and we allow Satan to convince us that we are incapable of entering. We dream of the day God will use us as the instrument of His will and the vessel through which His blessings will flow. Yet Satan through cunning mind tricks tries to convince us that we cannot accomplish the task that is set before us. He wants us to believe that we are unworthy of receiving the call to do God's will and receive His blessings.

The reason we allow these thoughts to be planted in our minds may be our insecurities, our history, or even our failures. The Scriptures remind us, however, that we truly can do God's will when we trust Him, lean on Him, and allow Him to work through us.

Just as a little girl depends upon her earthly father, we too can depend upon our heavenly Father. He loves us with an undying and an unwavering love. Indeed, God wants the very best for us. We are rich in talents, gifts, and abilities, and He wants to see us blossom and reach our fullest potential. Our meager minds cannot even imagine the depth of the blessedness that God intends for us.

Whenever you feel defeated, remember God has not given you the spirit of fear. Go to Him in prayer, admit your shortcomings, take time to listen to His guidance and direction, follow His will for your life, and above all, *don't quit!*

A Word of Encouragement to Sisters

Thought for the Day: Be all that you can be!

Scripture for the Day: *For God has not given us a spirit of fear, but of power and of love and of a sound mind. (2 Tim. 1:7)*

Patricia G. Thomas is the wife of the Reverend Dr. Walter S. Thomas, pastor of the New Psalmist Baptist Church of Baltimore, Maryland. She is a member of the International Association of Ministers' Wives and Ministers' Widows, Inc. and the Baptist Ministers' Wives and Ministers' Widows Alliance of Baltimore and Vicinity. She is also a contributing writer to *Seeds of Strength*. She is the mother of three children—Joi, Walter Jr., and Joshua. She serves as a disciple leader and lecturer to women.

Part 2

❧

Reflections on My Spiritual Journey

Look for the Bow

It was a rainy, chilly spring day. I sat with my head cupped in my hands at my dining room table. I was feeling overwhelmed and frustrated at the sudden challenges I was facing in my life. I had just completed my first year as pastor of a wonderful congregation. For the second time in less than a week I had buried a member of the parish—one of twenty that had passed during that year.

I sat there and thought about the pain of just getting to know people who are suddenly not there anymore. However, my reflection had to be brief, for I had just received a phone call that another member had died; the family was waiting for me at the church. Two other members were in intensive care units in separate hospitals. Another member was in a nursing home preparing to be taken to the emergency room. My own daughter had taken seriously ill. Meanwhile, my only living uncle lay in a coma in an ICU, and my family needed comfort.

My body was tired and I felt numb. My mind seemed too weary to think clearly, and I felt not as if the whole world were on my shoulders but as if it had been dropped like a slab of concrete on my whole body. I have never felt so helpless, hopeless, and alone in my life.

I prayed, "God, I don't want to be the strong woman and be all by myself; God, I need you. I don't want to save the world or be all things to all people; I need the strength of the Lord, God. I don't want to have a pity party; I need the joy of the Lord. God, please help me!

Suddenly, I felt a warmth and comfort flood my soul and my being. I lifted up my head and looked toward the sky. It had stopped raining. I saw not one but two rainbows. One reached across the East River and ended on my terrace. I cleared my eyes and saw the beautiful colors of yellow, lavender, green, blue, pink, among others, and I began to shout and leap for joy. For I remembered what God had told Noah: "When you see my bow in the cloud, you will know that never again will the world be destroyed with water" (Gen. 9:12–15, my paraphrase). I realized that this word was for me in my situation; that though trouble was flooding my soul I would not be destroyed for I had seen the "bow" of God in the clouds. Now, I was reminded that I would make it through the storm. No storm was to be everlasting, according to the Word of God.

Beloved, be encouraged if you are going through something difficult in your life. We are recipients of the promise; for God said when you see "My bow," the storm will be over. When the storm passes the rainbow must come out and it is the sign that God is with us. God is faithful. And nothing will ever overburden us to destruction. Look for the bow.

Thought for the Day: There is no rainbow without the rain.

Scripture for the Day: *Lo, I am with you always. (Matt. 28:20)*

The Reverend Carolyn Holloway is a native of North Carolina but has lived in New York City since the age of two. She is currently the senior pastor of the DeWitt

Reformed Church, located on the Lower East Side of Manhattan, where she presides over a vibrant, inner-city ministry. She is the first African-American woman pastor in DeWitt's 116 years. She was the recipient of the Benjamin E. Mays Award for 1990–92. She served as minister of outreach of the Mariners Temple Baptist Church under the pastorate of the Reverend Dr. Suzan Johnson Cook and was the associate executive director of Mariners' Multi-Ethnic Center Afterschool Program. Her other achievements include an internship in the Black Women in Ministry project sponsored by the NYC Mission Society; appointment to the federal steering committee for the African American Burial Ground in New York City; adjunct professor at the New York Theological Seminary; a contributing author to *Sister to Sister;* a council member of the African American Council of the RCA; and second vice president of the Manhattan Council of Churches. She is married and has four children.

The Match

That which you are seeking is seeking you.

When I saw a relatively small notice for a position at my stepdaughter's college, I knew that God was matching me with my perfect position. At the time, I was not looking to leave my job. My life's plan was set. I was going to remain at the college where I had come of age, professionally speaking, from lecturer to full professor and from associate dean to dean, until I reached retirement age.

The position was tailored to my background. Yet, with nearly thirty years of preparation, I almost let self-doubt resound louder than divine direction. "Step out on that skinny branch in faith and you will fly," was the message I kept receiving.

It was the second time in my life I knew I was being spiritually guided to a right place. The first time was when I met my husband. I wonder if I never met or married him, or if my stepdaughter had gone to another college, would I have ever noticed that ad.

If I told you that the day I responded to the notice and the day I met with my new college president to negotiate terms were only eight weeks apart, you too would recognize that God had been the headhunter for this position.

Life has become easier since I've learned not to resist that still, small voice that always guides me to the right place.

Thought for the Day: Step out in faith.

Reflections on My Spiritual Journey

Scripture for the Day: *Now faith is the substance of things hoped for, the evidence of things not seen. (Heb. 11:1)*

Dr. Ilona H. Anderson was appointed vice president of Academic Affairs and dean of faculty at Bloomfield College in Bloomfield, New Jersey, on July 1, 1997. She was also appointed as a tenured professor of humanities. Prior to this appointment, she had been serving as the acting dean of faculty relations at The City College of The City University of New York, where she was also a tenured member of the faculty. She now holds the title Professor Emeritus of English at The City College. Dr. Anderson is a member of Unity Church of Christ in Teaneck, New Jersey.

A Sister's Journey to the Motherland

Why the journey to Africa? During my chronological gift of forty plus years, personal evolution has focused my steps and choices. And as the thirst for knowledge about my origin grew, it called me to another level of my soul, to seek the root of who I am as an American of black African descent. My spirit sought connection to the soil of my ancestors, the beginning of our presence on the planet, to Africa's west coast city of Dakar, Senegal.

As I thoughtfully prepared for this personal pilgrimage the question arose: How did I want to honor the toils and triumphs of those Middle Passage survivors? Thinking about people and memories that have framed my life, I made a list of things to take on my sojourn. First came my deceased grandmother's watch, representing generational love and strength. Second, a Bible, a gift from my mother, symbolizing the time-tested salvation and wisdom of God. Third, a piece of wood my nephew gave me for Christmas about six years ago, when he was eight. (This bright, sensitive child touches my soul, and I wanted the collective embrace of our ancestors over him as he faces the world's challenges.) Last, a card from my college best friend, who has been a support to me for more than two decades. The card reads, "When God closes one door, he opens another."

I was now ready to visit one of the most significant landmarks of the world, Goree Island, situated in the backdrop of Dakar.

Remnants of its debatable and dark past confronted me from the outset with the slave castle accessible to the open Atlantic. Goree loomed formidable but open for healing. Entering and seeing the holding cells and iron shackles, the horror of the beginning of what is now the African-American story was revealed.

I took my four pilgrimage tokens, laid them out on the sacred soil, prayed, and cried. Moving on to the castle's "door of no return," and looking west over the Atlantic, the hymn "Amazing Grace" came to my lips. Thoughts surfaced about where I am now and where the hymn's author was as he penned those words. Change of heart, suffering, and triumph are all embodied in this hymn. Certainly, I may have once been lost, but I felt completely found at that moment—empowered, the spiritual segue between people and past made manifest. God's grace made it so.

Thought for the Day: Lord, it's good to be back home.

Scripture for the Day: *Therefore, since we are surrounded by so great a cloud of witnesses . . . let us run with endurance the race that is set before us. (Heb. 12:1)*

Deborah L. Parker is a human resource consultant, speaker, writer, and principal of DPJ Associates, a firm specializing in professional and personal development training programs and related services. Also a major in the U.S. Army Reserves, she speaks from experience on the topics of leadership, workforce diversity, career development, change management, and goal setting. Deborah has an M.A. in interdisciplinary studies from George Mason University and a B.A. in sociology from the College of William and Mary. Her community and professional memberships include Metropolitan Baptist Church in Washington, American Society for Training and Development, National Speakers Association, and National Council of Negro Women. She also serves as president of the Hulon Willis Association of the Society of the Alumni at the College of William and Mary.

He Lives in Me

When I said yes to Jesus, life became new; I then realized that God had really worked miraculously in me. The moral principles laid before me by my parents nurtured a desire in me to do all that I could to help others, especially the young, teaching them to have a personal relationship with Christ, who lives in all of them.

As I take inventory of my own gift of life, I thank God for Christian parents and teachers. It was in the City Point section of Hopewell, Virginia, that I found the Lord and confessed my faith. As I learned more about Jesus and the God of my salvation, I became a witness that God is real. He lives! He lives in me! I can't fully understand that fact with my mind, but my spirit understands, and I am committed to living out this reality and sharing it with others.

After I retired, through divine intervention, I found myself serving as associate minister of Ebenezer Missionary Baptist Church. My commitment to God was confirmed by order of ordination.

Christ is my inspiration, prayer is my work, and service is my contribution. I have learned to erase and replace—erase error and replace it with truth; erase fear and replace it with love. My salvation is my most precious possession. Christ has brought joy, peace, and unending blessing into my life.

Sharing and caring, interacting with others, and being divinely guided are a part of my belief. God works through a body, "and my soul shall be joyful in the LORD;/It shall rejoice in His salvation" (Ps. 35:9).

Thought for the Day: Count it all joy in Christ Jesus.

Scripture for the Day: *God willed to make known what are the riches of the glory of this mystery . . . which is Christ in you, the hope of glory. (Col. 1:27)*

Dr. Ruth Maness is a native of the City Point section of Hopewell, Virginia. There she graduated salutatorian of Carter G. Woodson High School in 1936. She has studied at Michigan State University and at the Billy Graham School of Evangelism, and in 1975 she received her Doctorate of Metaphysics from the Inter-Faith Society of Learning. She was ordained in 1962 in Brooklyn, New York. She has traveled to more than two hundred different countries and to five continents and has made seven Christian pilgrimages to the Holy City of Jerusalem. At age seventy-nine, Dr. Maness has reenrolled in theological studies, and is currently serving as minister, trustee, and Sunday school teacher at Ebenezer Missionary Baptist Church in Lansing, Michigan.

No More Yesterdays

When I can awaken each day—and not read about myself in the obituary column—I realize how blessed I am, for now I have another opportunity to begin again, to make a new start . . . a new mark.

The late Dr. Raymond Charles Barker often preached a sermon entitled "Yesterday Ended Last Night!"—a sermon that I have played over in my mind many times because it always reminded me that, at the crack of dawn, I have the opportunity to take a new page from life's diary and to begin to make new entries. This new day is destined to give me the opportunity to share life's experiences with others and, in essence, to reach back with a helping hand and lift someone up with me as I climb my Jacob's ladder.

St. Paul said, "I die daily" (1 Cor. 15:31). And it is in this dying to self—to negative thoughts, actions, and reactions—that I am able to find life with meaning. Each of us has that opportunity. When I have allowed yesterday to end last night, I find that I have left yesterday behind with all of its baggage. I am able to begin each day anew. I am able to live my life in the ever-present *now,* for God, who has brought me this far on life's journey, will see me through to the completion of my goals and dreams. All that I have to do is to "write the vision and make it plain" (Hab. 2:2).

On my spiritual journey, I have found that when I "let go and let God," He "is able to do exceeding abundantly above all that [I] ask or think" (Eph. 3:20). I extend to you, my sister, my hand of love. Take heart this day! Know that with God as your partner all things are possible. Only believe!

Thought for the Day: Let go and let God.

Scripture for the Day: *He who has begun a good work in you will complete it until the day of Jesus Christ. (Phil. 1:6)*

The Reverend Dr. Mary A. McCarthy was born in Brooklyn, New York, on 14 April 1929. She was educated in the New York City public school system. She was brought up in a Christ-centered home and, on 13 July 1980, she was ordained into the ministry. Dr. McCarthy is a graduate of Morgan State College (now "University"), Baltimore, Maryland, and of Teachers' College, Columbia University, in New York City. She is a mother of two (a son and a daughter), grandmother of four, and great-grandmother of two. She loves people and calls herself a "peacemaker" and an "encourager." She is a poet, writer, teacher, minister, and motivational speaker.

A Match Made in Heaven

Strength and dignity are her clothing and her position is strong and secure; she rejoices over the future [the latter day or time to come, knowing that she and her family are in readiness for it]! (Prov. 31:25 AMPLIFIED)

Prior to and during my marriage I heard various perspectives on marriage from friends, family, and spiritual leaders, yet no one could have ever prepared me for the challenges that awaited me in this ministry. I was unaware of some of the stages in a divine process that establishes holy and healthy marriages. I was also clueless about the hatred that Satan had for my husband, our marriage, and my commitment to Jesus Christ.

Trying experiences entered our marriage and threatened to shake the foundation of our faith in the Lord. My marital thorns were not unique, for many of my brothers and sisters also tasted the same trials but did not overcome them. A great number of them succumbed to the attacks and are found in mental wards, prisons, and graves. Depression, delirium, and death were not my destiny; holiness was. God gave me love, power, and a sound mind through it all. I was determined that I would not die physically or spiritually; instead, I would *live and declare the illustrious acts of the Lord.*

I learned to trust God like never before. My reliance on Him created a stir in hell and made me a spectacle for Christ. Some people, and certainly "spiritual hosts of wickedness in the heavenly places" (Eph. 6:12), underestimated the power of God at work in my life. The ability to take my positions, stand firm, and see the salvation of the Lord came from God alone. I said and did what God said and watched Him move. Although there were times I acted in the flesh, my God forgave and empowered me to continue in the race because my heart's desire was to be a woman of integrity. Christ continually assured me that He had given me the grace to endure and conquer what many others did not. Strengthened by God's Word and presence, I could remain in a place that some had concluded was a miserable state.

At any time I could have decided to do things my way, but I knew that my way meant spiritual death. I wanted what God wanted. I wanted to love what He loves and hate what He hates. It was God's way or no way. My circumstances were painful and frustrating, but my God was and still is greater than my circumstances. He says with all authority that "He Who lives in you is *greater* (mightier) than he who is in the world" (1 John 4:4 AMPLIFIED). Nothing was allowed to separate me from God's love. The Holy Spirit took me to new levels of faith, forgiveness, submission, prayer, peace, order, godliness, and commitment. He also gave me a better understanding of truth, life, love, and freedom. God could have changed the circumstances in my marriage, but He chose not to because He, being the Beginning and the End, knew the end. He had a purpose to not only deliver and heal us, but others around us too. Hallelujah!

The Holy Spirit was constantly telling me, "This is the way; walk in it, when you turn to the right hand and when you turn to the left" (Isa. 30:21 AMPLIFIED). He gave "the bread of adversity and the water of affliction," yet He never hid Himself (v. 21). Other Scriptures spoke directly to my heart and encouraged me to press on: "For you have not passed this way before" (Josh. 3:4). "Behold, I have refined you, but not as silver; I have tried and chosen you in the furnace of affliction" (Isa. 48:10 AMPLIFIED). "Fear not [there is nothing to fear], for I am with you; do not look around you in terror and be dismayed, for I am your God. I will strengthen and harden you to difficulties, yes, I will help you; yes, I will hold you up and retain you with My [victorious] right hand of rightness and justice" (Isa. 41:10 AMPLIFIED). "For I know the thoughts and plans that I have for you, says the Lord, thoughts and plans for welfare and peace and not for evil, to give you hope in your final outcome" (Jer. 29:11 AMPLIFIED).

What the enemy meant for evil became a springboard for personal and public deliverances. Comments and questions such as "Why stay?" and "*I* would leave" from people who heard my story were overshadowed by statements such as "Thank you for your witness, Sister Solomon; it has blessed more people than you know," and "Stephannie, you wear it well." Jesus accomplished much during this season of shaking: demons were *exposed, confronted,* and *cast down;* newly found godly weapons were *applied* like never before; ministry was *expanded;* and above all my love for Christ *increased.* In my most trying moments God gave me joy, wisdom, grace, mercy, smiles, laughter, fresh testimonies, and much more.

My husband and I were victorious in our season of adversity because God never abandoned us, and His blood remained on our marriage. Yes, I am a witness that the blood of Jesus obliterates anything that is against His way. Therefore, my sisters, trust God with all of your heart. With Him nothing is ever impossible and no word from Him shall be without power or impossible to fulfill. Choose to always walk by faith and not by sight and to believe only the report of the Lord.

Thought for the Day: Hang in there.

Scripture for the Day: *The genuineness of your faith, being much more precious than gold that perishes, though it is tested by fire, may be found to praise, honor, and glory at the revelation of Jesus Christ. (1 Peter 1:7)*

Stephannie Solomon authored the empowering book *Conversations with the King,* contributed to the inspiring publication *Sister to Sister: Devotions for and from African-American Women,* and has written monthly articles for *Unity in the Spirit* magazine's "In Response To" section. She has a

B.S. from Towson State University in elementary education and a master's degree in elementary and middle school mathematics from Morgan State University. She is a member of United Baptist Church in Baltimore, Maryland, with her husband, Pastor Carl J. Solomon, and their daughter, Sierra Simone.

Journey of a Lifetime

As I reflect on my spiritual journey, I reminisce about all the wonders of life, the new people I have met, and the places I have yet to discover. Before I began my journey, I was fearful, doubtful, confused, and weary. No matter what I did, I continued to live in darkness and despair, not knowing which way to turn.

But one day I surrendered my ego and my need to control things and I found myself wholeheartedly asking to receive Christ in my life. At that moment my life changed; I seemed to have been made over. It was almost as though I came alive for the first time. I am surrounded by love and filled with a perfect peace, one which I have never known. Through Bible study, motivational lectures, and fellowship I have come to understand that all that I am and all that I have is because of God, who has truly been my comforter and my salvation. God provides the light that guides my journey, even when I don't feel I can go on.

So, my sisters, when you are ready to move forward, pack up your baggage, pick up your marching orders, and find yourself on the journey of a lifetime. You can be sure that your spiritual journey will outlive this earthly stay.

Thought for the Day: Today, I am ready for my marching orders.

Scripture for the Day: *In Him was life, and the life was the light of men. (John 1:4)*

Lorraine Cambridge lives in Mt. Vernon, New York. A devout Christian and a college graduate, she currently works as a New York City Probation Officer in Bronx County. She enjoys mentoring, being with family, and traveling.

Me and a Man Named Job

In the first chapter of the book of Job, a wealthy man's faith is tested when he loses his family, friends, and all his worldly possessions. The wonderful part is that over the next forty-two chapters that man never loses his faith in God, and he proves to be a man of great faith.

There are many lessons in Job—lessons about patience, fear, anger, and love. Job's story is a classic because it teaches us how to face and overcome our problems.

As I reflect on my life, I see many comparisons between Job's life and mine. I, too, have had pain and suffering. Over time

I've learned to trust God and not to lean on my own understanding.

In my earlier years I always strove for perfection. I tried to excel in everything. In my world you were expected to perform at 150 percent all the time, to be your own best friend, and to believe in yourself. So I did. It was my downfall because after applying all my talent and all my effort, I still failed. Then my life took a 180-degree turn, and instead of trusting in myself, I was led to turn to the Lord. Learning to surrender my will has been very difficult, but I'm learning and it's getting easier each day.

I'm not a biblical scholar, nor do I profess to be an evangelist, but I do have a testimony. My hardheadedness caused me a lot of pain along the way. When I started surrendering my will to the Lord, I saw many of my burdens lifted. Problems were solved, people's hearts changed toward me, and the fear that had forever haunted me began to fade. I'm so glad to be a child of the King.

Thought for the Day: I am facing my problems by placing my problems in God's hands.

Scripture of the Day:
If a man dies, shall he live again?
All the days of my hard service I will wait,
Till my change comes. (Job 14:14)

Santa Rose Scott resides in Westchester, New York. She is the proud mother of Angela and a grandmother of two. She is glad to be a child of the King.

God's Plans, Not Mine

Scripture tells us that God has a plan for us, to give us a future and a hope (Jeremiah 29:11 NIV). This message was initially given to Jeremiah to encourage the captives in Babylon to move ahead and pray for those who enslaved them. I am learning to accept this as a personal message for me, from God, to let go and let God be God.

I am reminded of the anxieties I experienced during some recent recording projects. I created these anxieties because of my impatience—not letting go and letting God be God. I was very disappointed with the lack of progress as I watched the completion dates continue to slip, mainly because I had no control of the outcome. I realized I needed to practice what I had been preaching: *let go and trust God.*

I was reminded of a quote: "God does not have to provide anything we can't trust Him for."[1] Allowing God to work at the details has never been one of my strongest qualities. Isn't it interesting that no matter how confident in God's agenda we pretend to be, we still get upset when God doesn't follow *our* plan? I am learning I can either trust God, let go, and find peace or I can carry the burden of the disappointments and anxieties and be miserable.

Do you find yourself trying to control situations by moving ahead of God's schedule? Let go, pray, and find peace by trusting God to do what is best for you.

Thought for the Day: Order my steps, Lord.

Reflections on My Spiritual Journey

Scripture for the Day: *In all your ways acknowledge Him, And He shall direct your paths. (Prov. 3:6)*

Linda Fay Harris is an ordained deaconess of the New Psalmist Baptist Church in Baltimore, Maryland. She is married to her business manager, Larry Harris. They have one son, Lance Michael. Linda is a "psalmist" of a special music ministry, recording artist, producer and consultant to other aspiring artists, and a workshop facilitator. She graduated in 1998 from Johns Hopkins University with a master's in applied behavioral science. She has been employed at AlliedSignal Communications Systems since 1979.

1. Rogers, M.C. and C.V. King, *The Kingdom Agenda: Experiencing God in Your Workplace* (Murfreesboro, TN: Saratoga Press, 1996).

Part 3

❧

The Blessings in My Life

Mother's Business

The movie *Soul Food* reminded me of the blessings of family in all of its many forms. Like the siblings in that movie, we recently lost the last remaining parent in our family. We were all wondering as is often the case, "How do we cope, Lord?"

My mother-in-law, Louvenia Brown, was a pillar of strength for our family. She married a young widower with two very small children. Over the course of forty-three years together they built two successful businesses as well as a strong foundation based on love, sharing, and commitment.

My earliest memories of her were about the simple things that, upon reflection, make up the fabric of a relationship. My husband and I would, on occasion, stop to see his parents after work. As a young married woman who could not cook, I was amazed at the dishes that magically appeared on the table after only a half hour of preparation!

Discussions were always lively, and after dinner we would clean up, relax, and head back home to prepare for the next day. When our first child was born, my mother and my mother-in-law were both there to share in the experience. Unfortunately, my mother did not live to see my daughter's first birthday, but my mother-in-law was there for me in her own very quiet way; whether filling the need for a baby-sitter or sending dinner . . . again so simple yet profound in the comfort it provided. When my own daughter-in-law was fatally stricken, my mother-in-law, despite her illness, was our gentle guide and presence.

There are so many memories; so many single threads; so many wonderful lessons learned that as I ask again, "How do we cope?" I have come to believe that her answer would be, "I've shown you the way; now go about Mother's business."

Thought for the Day: Thank God for the mothers in your life. They are gifts from God.

Scripture for the Day:
Wherever you go, I will go;
And wherever you lodge, I will lodge;
Your people shall be my people,
And your God, my God. (Ruth 1:16)

Gladys Brown is an assistant vice president at Citibank N.A. and is currently a part of the Business Testing Unit in Global

Finance Operations and Technology. Prior to joining Citibank in 1965, Gladys attended the Fashion Institute of Technology, where she majored in apparel design and merchandising. She and her husband have two children and two grandchildren. She is a member of St. Pascal Baylon R.C. Church, where she lectures and is involved in the parish council. She represents her parish at the diocesan level on the Committee for Racial Harmony and the Public Policy Network. She is also an active member of the New York Coalition of 100 Black Women and the Urban Bankers' Coalition.

Uncommon Favor

After many years of getting from God exactly what I asked for, I have reluctantly concluded that I have uncommon favor with Him. Often friends and family have jokingly asked me to introduce them to my God. But the Christians among them already know Him. The difference is faith.

It took me a long time to realize that, indeed, that is what it is. Every time I ask God for something, I ask expecting an answer. The moment I finish my prayer, I am convinced that it is done. I have even gotten into the habit of thanking Him in advance for answering my prayers.

When something disappointing, hurtful, or unjust happens in my life, I try to spend little time in the very human side of me that hurts easily because I know that the disappointment has just set me up for another of God's miracles. I know in my heart that God wants me healthy, happy, and successful. So when things don't go as I wish, by faith I know that what God is going to give to me must be more incredible than what I thought I wanted.

In turn, the more I expect from Him, the more He gives me; and the more He gives me, the more He expects from me. The more I give back, the more blessings I receive. The more my faith increases, the more opportunities He gives me to increase my faith.

I, therefore, place myself in the position of receiving His uncommon favor, which means my needs are anticipated, my desires are considered, and my prayers are answered.

Thought for the Day: God is only a prayer away, but those who come to God must believe that God *is*.

Scripture of the Day: *Whatever things you ask when you pray, believe that you receive them, and you will have them. (Mark 11:24)*

Felicia D. Henderson is co-executive producer of the Warner Brothers series *Sister, Sister*. Other television writing credits include *Moesha, The Fresh Prince of Bel Air,* and *Family Matters.* Henderson has a B.A. from UCLA and an M.B.A. from the University of Georgia. She is currently enrolled in the M.F.A. program in UCLA's School of Film & Television, where she is finishing her first screenplay. One of eight children,

Henderson grew up in Pasadena, California, where she currently resides. With eighteen nieces and nephews and seven great nieces and nephews, Henderson is very committed to being a role model and mentor.

Share the Music

I have always believed that music is a gift from God. He has planted in every one of us a need to lift our voices in song—a desire to sing low, to sing a sweet lullaby until the innocent child sleeps. We do not need voice lessons to meet this desire unless our need to sing blossoms so fully that we are compelled to open the door to a life full of singing—sometimes for Jesus, sometimes for the world.

I attended my first voice class more than thirty-five years ago. Because I had an exceptional teacher, her valuable lessons continue to ricochet across my mind.

First I learned to sing for my supper, and then I, too, became a voice teacher. For more than twenty-five years, I have instructed many dozens of professional and nonprofessional singers. Some became famous; some did not.

My fondest memory, however, is of my very first voice student, Suzan Johnson, a tall, sensitive twelve year old from the Bronx. I was delighted she came to me so that I could instill in her the skills needed to lift her voice and touch people. This was her dream. But because her gifts were vast and her parents supported her in fields other than music, I lost her as a student. Nevertheless, one of my greatest blessings is that some of my students have become permanent players on the stage of my life.

While Suzan, now the Reverend Dr. Suzan Johnson Cook, is a superstar in religion and politics, and I continue to teach, arrange, and write music, something very gentle, something very quiet continues to motivate us to reach out to each other. We are two African-American women, one younger, one older, each compelled to share the music and to forever sing the God-given song of life.

Thought for the Day: You have a song within you. Sing your song of life.

Scripture of the Day:
Oh, sing to the L*ORD* *a new song!*
For he has done marvelous things. (PS. 98:1)

Pat Holley began her career in music as a cabaret artist, playing and singing a vast repertoire of standard song compositions and popular hits. She has taught vocal technique, coached, and worked in various musical capacities with recording star Stephanie Mills; Metropolitan Opera star Shirley Verrett; supermodel Iman; principal stars of *Mama, I Want To Sing;* original rapper Doug E. Fresh; gospel singing star Shirley Hopkins; Tony Award winners and nominees Hinton Battle, Ernestine Jackson, and Lillias White; and other singers, both professional and nonprofessional. She has logged hundreds of hours in recording studios as a record producer and arranger. Her latest project is *Heart Song,* a new musical for which she has written the lyrics, book, and music. Ms. Holley studied composition and arranging at The Juilliard School and City College of New York. She is married and lives on Manhattan's Upper West Side.

Part 4

❧

Finding Out What Really Matters

That Roller Coaster Ride Called Life

I thought I knew what it took to make me happy and what it meant to be happy. I thought I was in control. When trained in corporate gamesmanship, one can develop a cavalier, arrogant, overconfident attitude that sends the message that you're in control. I found out that I didn't have a clue what it was to be happy (joyous) or in control. A series of events in my life brought me to that jolting realization.

I can remember that day in March 1989 as if it were yesterday. I had gotten up early to get a jump on the day. As a bank officer at a very large New York City money center bank, my first business meeting of the day was at 7:00 A.M., and I would be moving through my schedule quickly and steadily until midnight. I was a workaholic.

At 2:00 A.M., my oldest son, Mark, had dropped by to check on me. He ended up taking me to a hospital emergency ward. The ER staff checked my blood pressure, heart rate, etc. They were okay. But the doctors couldn't explain my inability to walk a straight line. No, I was not drunk. They summoned a neurologist, ran tests, and discovered a brain tumor. I was admitted, prepped, and underwent a five-and-a-half-hour operation within the next two days. Just like that! I hadn't a clue that I would end up in the hospital that morning. Who was in control? God showed who was in complete control. God got my attention. He slam-dunked me into reality.

I was frightened and unprepared for death. I wasn't saved at the time and had no relationship with God. While in the hospital, I called on those I knew who prayed and asked for their prayers. I remember calling the Reverend Suzan Johnson, who was not my pastor at that time. We were acquainted through civic organizations in which we were both involved. She prayed with me, and her prayers gave me great comfort.

I left the hospital in ten days. The doctors were surprised and delighted by my rate of recovery. I entered that hospital with patients that were still there when I left.

My life changed after being spared by God's grace. All the things that I had thought were so important for my children and me paled in light of my newfound spiritual life. I found out what really matters. God! Family! Love! You will do well at any career, job, or endeavor if you keep these things first in your life. These priorities should be your driving force.

I gave my life to Christ soon after coming out of the hospital. I began to take the time to appreciate people and things that I used to take for granted. How loving and protective my sons, Mark and Ayodele, were to me. How sweet the flowers smelled, how wonderful the sun felt on my face, how beautiful the trees were. I began to take more time with my immediate family, and they saw changes in me. They saw me willingly accept Christ as my savior. They saw my prayer and devotional life evolving. My relationships with them began to change also. Things that used to irritate me no longer irritated me. They were insignificant in comparison to the life-threatening ordeal I had just experienced. I found out what really matters.

The things that captured my attention—

career pressures, a big salary, upward mobility, business contacts, financial responsibilities—were all secularly based. All during my career I had neglected my spiritual life and lost sight of what really mattered. I knew about spirituality, but I hadn't pursued it. All that changed after my illness. Now I'm upwardly mobile for Christ.

While recovering, I felt deeply that God was preparing me for something important by giving me this second chance. In December 1993 I found out what it was. My younger sister called and asked if I'd accompany her to her doctor's office to receive the results of X rays she had taken. She was nervous and scared. Her worst fears were realized. The test results showed that she had lung cancer. The tumor the doctor found was so large that it completely engulfed the right lung.

The roller coaster ride began that day for

us. My being her closest relative meant that I would be transporting her back and forth to the hospital for the massive doses of chemotherapy that would leave her violently ill after each treatment.

Her oncologist dispassionately told me one day that she had approximately seven months to live. Her primary doctor had treated her for bronchitis for more than a year without detecting the seriousness of her condition. My sister smoked heavily and had been in denial that her condition was as bad as it was. When she finally decided to take X rays, the disease was too advanced to treat effectively. The chemotherapy didn't shrink the tumor, and neither did the subsequent radiation treatments.

I remember running to my church's prayer meeting every week during that period of my life. I was a member of Mariners' Temple Baptist Church, where

Suzan Johnson Cook was pastor. There I received the strength and support I needed to care for my sister.

I had to be strong for both of us. My sister became depressed and wanted to give up, but I kept praying that God would keep her with us a little longer because I couldn't accept the separation just yet. *Just a little longer, Jesus. Just a little longer*.

I was working full time and caring for my sister on the weekends. The rigors of our routine were taking a physical and emotional toll on me. Finally I made a decision to step out on faith. I quit my full-time job and took charge of my sister's affairs. If I hadn't had my own spiritual awakening in 1989, I wouldn't have willingly made the sacrifice for my sister in 1994. God is awesome. Through prayer, family, and my church family God stretched the seven months that the oncologist had predicted into sixteen months.

As with many adult family members, my sister and I hadn't been close since childhood. But during daily contact, with my having to take care of her, we began to recall our childhood experiences, especially some of the funny and crazy things we had done in our youth. (I wonder why we wait so long before reconnecting with our loved ones.) I placed my sister in a hospice in March 1995, and she went home to God in April 1995.

My God of second chances had shown me once again the blessings in my life and what really mattered.

As a youth my favorite amusement park ride was the roller coaster because of the rush I received on that first drop. Now that I'm on my Christian walk, I find that same sensation in serving the Lord Jesus Christ, the ultimate rush!

Thought for the Day: God will give you many

chances. Take hold of the opportunities He places in front of you before it is too late.

Scripture for the Day: *By His stripes we are healed. (Isa. 53:5)*

Coral C. Aubert, an executive in the banking industry for twenty-five years and business consultant, received her business degree from Pace University. She is now on the staff of Bronx Christian Fellowship Church as office manager. Ms. Aubert is also part of the church's leadership team. She has worked with at-risk youth and adults in a training program in Harlem and has been involved in the lives of homeless children. Her volunteerism spans more than forty-five years.

Family Before Fame

My parents knew I would be in the public eye early on. I was a ham at the age of two, mimicking people I saw on television, especially singer Tom Jones.

As a teenager I wanted fame, and I spent a lot of time thinking of ways to be known internationally. It happened. I broke into the business at age eighteen. I began as a radio DJ then became a news anchor and news director. Then the big time—a White House correspondent with an office located at 1600 Pennsylvania Avenue, making me one of the few people achieving this status.

While struggling and reaching the so-called top, something was missing. I was missing the biggest events; events with my father, mother, brother, and my extended family. I also did not have enough time to work on a stronger April or to learn who I was. I wanted children and a husband, but I was not ready. With no sense of self, I was going through the motions while putting everything on hold.

Sometimes facing yourself is the hardest thing to do. In the last few years, I decided to get a grip on my life and rediscover my family. My recipe: reflecting on the strength of my roots and my religious background and renewing my faith and my love for the Lord.

It started falling into place. I began finding joy in the small things, such as gardening, which was a passion of my late grandmother. I also found a peace that did not make me want to run and be on the go all the time. I discovered that I had been running from the pain of seeing the real me, alone and a loner. What really mattered was to reach out and be a part of my family once again and not go through a dress rehearsal. I am glad for my accomplishments but thankful for the blessings of family.

Thought for the Day: Take a day, or two, to sit alone with God and rediscover what really matters.

Scripture for the Day: *For what profit is it to a man if he gains the whole world, and loses his own soul? (Matt. 16:26)*

April Danielle Ryan, a twelve-year journalism veteran, has been a White House correspondent for American Urban Radio Networks (AURN) since January 1997. Along with daily responsibilities at the

White House, Ryan hosts the daily feature, "The White House Report," which is broadcast on AURN's nearly three hundred affiliated stations nationwide. Prior to working for AURN, Ryan worked for several radio stations in Baltimore, including V103, where she was news director. Ryan has conducted interviews with President Clinton, Mrs. Clinton, and Vice President Gore. Ryan was named one of the Outstanding Young Women in America for 1997–98. The Baltimore native is a graduate of Morgan State University.

The Loss of a Dear Friend

Though we've skated along that thin ice,
leaning to and fro,
Never expecting those we loved dearly,
to pass or cease to go.

There's nothing more devastating
than the loss of a dear friend.
For life becomes less tasteful,
when a relationship just ends.

Nothing lasts forever,
Their temporary gifts, of our present time,
planted every season.

To taste of all their goodness
makes life so much more pleasing.

Without their sweet aroma,
we lay loose, in bitter cold.
And we can't go through the wilderness of grief,
alone and spiritually not whole.

There are no words in our dictionaries
to express our tragic loss.
Those ties and associations were imperative;
they were our background force.

Grounded in grinds of pitiful regret,
now crushed, we can't forget.
For we're haunted by their memory,
we're suffering and obsessed.

So treasure all those roots of time,
which have bonded you together.
For life was not unfair.
Give Him thanks along the way,

for His purpose was solely to
teach us all to truly share.

Let His gentle breeze blow through your mind,
as we lift Him up in prayer each day.
Enjoying the freshness of His spirit
will help those mourns of misery
slowly fade away.
Then, Celebrate, Celebrate those losses,
for He'll plant new seeds of friendships
if we trust and then obey.

Disconnected from our Soul Mate,
our dear friend has departed.
Into the fields of no return,
with God, *is where we started.*

Thought for the Day: It's good to have true friends.

Scripture for the Day: *Love suffers long and is kind; love does not envy; love does not parade itself, is not puffed up. (1 Cor. 13:4)*

Agnes Cambridge is a down to earth single parent and devoted mother of two. Originally a New Yorker, she is now living in Houston, Texas. At the peak of an exciting career, she has decided to touch base with people who need to be inspired through her inspirational poetry.

Winning

America places so much emphasis on winning. If we are not number one, we are not fulfilling the American standard. Well, I'm here to tell you, sisters, that you can always win, but you must listen to the small, inner (positive) voice that directs you. Here's my journey.

At the beginning of 1998 I was privileged to be selected to compete in a major vocal competition. During the week of the competition, feeling nervous and anxious and practicing every chance I got, I was very determined and felt confident that I could win. When my name was not called to go to the next round, I cried and called my mother and sister for encouragement and spiritual uplifting. Naturally, I felt better after talking to them. The next day the judges at the vocal competition gave all the contestants feedback. I found out where my strengths were, and I also discovered which areas needed strengthening. After talking with the judges, I felt even better—I was close to being selected (thank you, Jesus!)—and was rejuvenated and challenged to compete the next year. I also realized that I may not have won that competition, but I was a winner just being there.

To me, winning is constantly humbling yourself before God and asking Him for understanding, clarity, and courage to analyze your actions so that you can win that next competition, job interview, game, relationship, court case—life in general—and understanding that blessings come even in feedback. Winning is also planning your course of action instead of doing everything at the last minute. I am a winner, and you are too.

Thought for the Day: Try, try again.

Scripture for the Day: *I press toward the goal for the prize of the upward call of God in Christ Jesus. (Phil. 3:14)*

Pamela Ruby Babb is a soprano member of the Grace Bumbry Spiritual Ensemble and a soloist in the Forever Amen Ensemble of the Abyssinian Baptist Church in Harlem. She also works at The Harlem School of the Arts as director of marketing, public and government relations. She is a graduate of Hampton University in Virginia, Columbia University, New York City, and the High School of Music and Art (now the LaGuardia School for the Performing Arts) in Manhattan.

Cast Your Net into the Deep

I believe that God made us in his image, three-fold: body, soul, and spirit—external, internal, and eternal—physical, mental, and spiritual. I have discovered something in the Bible that has worked in my life, making me a better person, and I believe it will make you a better person too.

The Bible was written for us with directions on how the blessings will unfold. In its pages we learn that God in His divine wisdom and goodness gave each of us gifts to be developed. We have the power to become great. It is up to each of us to study and show ourselves approved (2 Timothy 2:15 KJV).

It is wrong to blame others for what we do not know and for what we do not have: "You do not have because you do not ask" (James 4:2). Luke 5:5 says that Peter had fished all night and caught nothing until Jesus helped him. Like Peter, many of us have been from one learning experience to another—church, school, and job—with no directions. In Peter's case, when divine directions came, he cast his net into the deep and was blessed. We need to listen for and obey those same divine directions at all times, but especially when we lose our way.

Trust God. Know that the Christ in you is your hope of glory (Colossians 1:27). God's Word is the road map. It is our path, our way.

Thought for the Day: On my own I can do nothing. With Christ I can do all things.

Finding Out What Really Matters

Scripture for the Day: *Your word is a lamp to my feet And a light to my path. (Ps. 119:105)*

Dr. Ruth Powell Maness is a native of the City Point section of Hopewell, Virginia. There she graduated salutatorian of Carter G. Woodson High School in 1936. She has studied at Michigan State University and at the Billy Graham School of Evangelism, and in 1975, she received her Doctorate of Metaphysics from the Inter-Faith Society of Learning. She was ordained in 1962 in Brooklyn, New York. She has traveled to more than two hundred different countries and to five continents and has made seven Christian pilgrimages to the Holy City of Jerusalem. At age seventy-nine, Dr. Maness has reenrolled in theological studies, and is currently serving as minister, trustee, and Sunday school teacher at Ebenezer Missionary Baptist Church in Lansing, Michigan.

Finding Meaning in a Nontraditional Life

For a long time I felt as if I was always playing catch-up with my peers. What did they know that I didn't, I wondered. What secret did they have for sailing smoothly over all of life's hurdles? I would admonish myself, saying, "When are you going to get it together? By the time you finish college, get married, and have children, you'll be thirty." And with every birthday the age got pushed back further, and further, and further. "Will I ever be able to buy a house? Do I have to double or triple what I didn't save in my twenties so that I can match what financial gurus say I should have in my still unopened IRA?" Forget about the biological clock; I had so many other clocks ticking in my head I was about to go cuckoo.

Over the years I have met many women like me. Our churches and communities are filled with women who dwell on what they do not have.

Today is the day to bring peace to your soul. I understand clearly now that psalm taught in Sunday school. "He maketh me to lie down in green pastures" (Ps. 23:2 KJV). Too often we go through life worried that we are missing something when we have not learned to embrace what we have.

God makes us stop in green pastures because like sheep we would not have wisdom to know all is well. "The LORD is my shepherd; I shall not want" (v. 1). True meaning in life comes from a close walk with God. Peace is the fruit of service and faith to what you have. Like me, your life may not be on the timeline set by society, but, praise God, everyone's cross and crown has been made to order for a custom fit.

Thought for the Day: God's time is always on time.

Scripture for the Day:
Surely goodness and mercy shall follow me
All the days of my life;
And I will dwell in the house of the LORD
Forever. (Ps. 23:6)

Weptanomah Carter Davis is a weekly advice columnist for *The Baltimore Times* and a career and life counselor. She has a B.S. from the University of Maryland and an M.S. in counseling psychology from Loyola College, Baltimore, Maryland. In addition, she has her certificate of study in alcohol and substance abuse counseling. She has worked in various mental health settings and is currently the coordinator for a single-parent grant in Bergen County, New Jersey. Along with her mother, Dr. Weptanomah W. Carter, she is the coeditor of the book *Seeds of Strength* and coauthor of the book *She Said, She Said*. She is married to Dr. Henry P. Davis III, pastor of the Second Canaan Baptist Church, New York City. They have one daughter.

The Two Commandments

We in the Western Hemisphere have had to pay a high price in order to create a society based on Judeo-Christian ethics.

Through the centuries we have kept the faith following the two commandments of Christ Jesus: loving God and loving our neighbors the way we love ourselves (Matthew 22:37–39). Now society is changing at an alarming pace, and two very destructive forces are taking center stage: deceit and indifference, like "the bitter clamor of two eager tongues."[1]

It was said long ago that "deceit is gross impiety."[2] Indeed, deception goes against the very nature of God; He is truth. And indifference exemplifies the mark of Cain: "Am I my brother's keeper?" (Gen. 4:9). Of course, God intended him to be just that.

Our history reminds us of the promises of our God. We need only turn around and follow the two great commandments given to us by Christ Jesus, enjoy life with all the splendor of the African mystique, and realize that all of God's blessings are forever.

1. William Shakespeare, *King Richard II*, Act I, Scene 1, line 49.
2. From the Latin, *Es sumnum nefas fallere.*

Thought for the Day: Today is my day to love.

Scripture for the Day: *For all the law is fulfilled in one word, even in this: "You shall love your neighbor as yourself." (Gal. 5:14)*

Vernie Ellis is a retired nurse administrator with a background in geriatrics. She is active in politics and has held the position of county committee member and vice president of the Essex County League of Women Voters. She has had appointments to the East Orange Public Libraries Board of Trustees and the Library Science Construction Act Advisory Council. She is also a member of the East Orange Board of Health, Iota Phi Lambda Sorority Inc., and the nongovernment organization United Nations Department of Public Information. She and her husband have one son, two daughters, and two granddaughters.

The Way I Am

The dearest gift I give
Is love for my
Fellow man.

This love is deep
And endures and is
Always near at hand.

I give myself
Without the fear of
Being ridiculed

And think not
Of prejudice against
My curious self.

For there are those
Who do not know
Why I am the
Way I am.

I do not always
Meet broad smiles
And love along
My way.

I don't accept
The negative but
Give a smile instead.

For they don't
Understand the way

I am and why I'm
Not like them.
So with my
Smile in place
I travel along
My way.

Never deterred
By the negative man
I stay the
Course to the end.

Now here I am
Still full of love
For those less
Loved than I.

And knowing how
Fortunate I am
I keep my love inside

And cherish those
Who understand
The soul I have
Inside.

Thought for the Day: Find your gift, knowing that it comes from God.

Scripture for the Day: *The greatest of these is love. (1 Cor. 13:13)*

Marjorie E. Johnson was born in Kingston, Jamaica, and has lived in the United States for the past thirty-six years. She is a divorced mother of one daughter. She is an administrative assistant in the Human Development and Reproductive Health Unit at the Ford Foundation in New York. She enjoys reading, the arts, and writing poetry.

Part 5

Tapping into That Spiritual Strength

My Finest Year

With my gym bag, my Bible, and my American Express card, there I was on the street. There wasn't much that separated me and the other homeless lady on the subway, except that I own a house in New Jersey, an apartment in New York, and a winter place in Miami, Florida. I also proudly possess two undergraduate degrees and one master's degree and have been in the right social circles, the women's groups Links and Jack and Jill. I was considered a comfortable, middle-class black woman. So why was I alone with no place to go?

And worst of all, why did I have to run away from my home in the middle of the night? Why did I have to call 911 and scream for help? *He hit me. He choked me.* There, I said it, and I'm still okay.

We were practically newlyweds, having been married not quite four years. Yet this night was not the first time he had hit me. There were other times that he was violent. Those first few times I had thought to myself, *I can handle this. I'm strong, confident and in charge. He won't hit me again; he loves me.*

I recalled the time when he did not speak a word to me for six weeks. I talked to myself and started working late hours to avoid the loud silence. I kept telling myself, *This isn't real. I don't fit the mold of an abused wife.* When I was growing up, my models were women who were educated, strong, moral, independent, and God-fearing. My father was a brilliant man, an entrepreneur who treated my mom like a queen; he even called her "Madame Queen." In my home, there were no drugs, no fighting. There were summer vacations at the Jersey shore and on Martha's Vineyard. My life experience did not include men like the one I had married.

I asked myself, *Why me? I love this man.* The question that I should have asked is, Why not me? Why should I be exempt from the tests and trials of life? I began to ask, Do I love me? Do I love the Lord? Do I really know and believe that I am always in His care and protection? Do I believe that He will give me all I need to cope with the idea of being homeless and of having to get a protection order to separate me from the violent man I married?

It has been a year since I ran from my home late in the night. First I lived in a temporary space, then a rented room, now my own apartment, all with the court's protection order in my purse.

Looking back, I consider this year one of the best years of my life because I held on to "God's unchanging hand" and I found me. I learned, that I, like the homeless lady on the subway, am simply a child of God.

Thought for the Day: I am important to God.

Scripture for the Day: *We are hard-pressed on every side, yet not crushed; we are perplexed, but not in despair. (2 Cor. 4:8,9)*

Cathy Woods-Bristow was born and raised in Pittsburgh, Pennsylvania. She began taking courses at the University of Pittsburgh in sixth grade. She graduated from Wheelock College in Boston as part of a pilot project to integrate women's colleges on the East Coast. She later received a nursing degree from UCLA, which enabled her to start a Lamaze business in the early '70s. She also received an MBA from Pepperdine. She currently lives in Harlem, New York, and attends Caanan Baptist Church. She has one daughter. She recently divorced the man she wrote about here.

Going Through

For all those who have, are, or will be "going through," be encouraged! I share the following, that God is faithful when we are weak.

Too many times when I was feeling spiritually, emotionally, and mentally weak, abused and/or traumatized, I would be approached with spiritual compromise. It wasn't the unsaved that were the real problem, but the saved; those who were compromising their own spiritual maturity and authority.

Those times in my life were not easy. But then again, who said life would be easy? As we see with Jesus, his greatest temptation for spiritual compromise came after He had been fasting and was weak (Luke 4:1–14).

In my trials I felt as if I was being buried alive under tons of cement. But God merely was putting the focus of my trust to the test. Those who were being inappropriate were also being tested, but it was for me to pass or fail the test. Who would *always* be *my* spiritual authority, God or man? Whose approval would I seek, God's or man's? Whose definition of right and wrong would I trust, God's or man's? This was the test that would either break me or make me.

Each time I felt that I had one foot over the abyss of the valley of no return. I didn't have the strength to stop, but I had the sincere desire to say no. And when I weakly whispered no in my soul, God snatched me back into His arms and gave me the strength to cry out boldly, NO! NOT SO!

I conclude with a victory poem I wrote for myself. After you've "gone through," maybe you'll write a victory poem for yourself!

I was conceptualized in God's mind and
Conceived in God's womb. God took
Breath, ruach, from out of
God's own self and ordained my existence.
I am not haphazard or an afterthought. I have been custom built!
From God's own specifications. There is none
Other quite like me. I take my place as one
Of God's masterpieces, of El's own handiwork.
I am beautiful, because beauty is in the eye of the beholder
And it is God who first beheld me!

Thought for the Day: Victory shall be mine!

Scripture for the Day: *See, I have set the land before you; go in and possess the land which the* LORD *swore to your fathers. (Deut. 1:8)*

Shelia Maria Wilson was born in Cleveland, Ohio, the only child of Ida and Dave H. Wilson. She received a B.S. degree in education from Ohio State University. She received her M.Div. from the Colgate Rochester Divinity Schools in 1990 and a master's degree in religious education from there in 1994. She was ordained by the American Baptist Churches, USA, and is currently a chaplain in the U.S. Air Force.

Not What You Want, but What You Are Supposed to Have!

God is the Master Manager! Managers are trained to have staff buy into an idea, creating a feeling of ownership. There is no tangible ownership. What we are really talking about is authorship, feeling that your input counts and directly affects the decision making.

Well, at thirty, I have completely bought into myself. God has given me authorship, and my life is my own. I always know what I want and know I should have it. I usually make sound decisions. But when I turned thirty, I got a little ahead of the Manager's plan.

I knew I wanted Mr. Right, two beautiful children, a home, a car, and a good life. So I revisited a relationship with my former fiancé, thinking that if he had once been my fiancé, he must be *almost* right. Some time had passed; maybe he was ready now, I thought. We reconnected and went through all the motions and emotions. He started giving me mixed signals. I attributed his noncommittal behavior to fear. Then God revealed to me that his actions were because of another woman, eight months pregnant with his child. He had committed to marrying her while seeing me. He has never admitted any of this. I believe God allowed me to find out to keep me from making a decision that would have ultimately hurt me.

Painful as it was, I was thankful for God's intervention. I felt protected and blessed. God gives us authorship so that we feel good about ourselves and our decisions. But like a good manager, He steps in when necessary and takes control.

Thought for the Day: God is the Master Manager. Always follow His lead.

Scripture for the Day:
Trust in the LORD *with all*
your heart,
And lean not on your own
understanding. (Prov. 3:5)

Alicia Vernell Fields, a motivational self-empowerment and personal development specialist, is an activist for women and entrepreneurship. As the founder and CEO of Vernell Communications, Alicia hosts the Monthly Business Brunch, a gathering in support of entrepreneurs and aspiring entrepreneurs of color. In addition, she is the primary facilitator for the Soul to Soul Sisters Retreat, a weekend getaway for women conducive to retrospect, recreation, and rejuvenation. Alicia received her bachelor of arts degree in communications from Hampton University. She is a graduate of the Columbia Business School, Institute for Not-for-Profit Management, Rutgers University, Leadership Management for Urban Executives Institute, and is certified by Educational Designs that Generate Excellence (EDGE) to train youth in entrepreneurship.

"Pain Is Good"

Working out is painful. But doing so regularly has its benefits. Medical experts agree that the more you exercise, the less your risk of contracting debilitating or life-threatening diseases. Building muscle and burning fat, they say, are catalysts for a healthier life.

I'm a working out sistah! There was a time when I had no pep in my step, no glide in my stride, and worst of all, there was a hole in my soul! When I finally realized how much healthier I could be if I shed my excess baggage, I got to steppin'!

"Give me twenty more! . . . Hold on! . . .

You can do it! . . . Pain is good!" yells my fitness trainer. Yes. Pain is good.

Pain can make you holler for Jesus, and He'll awaken your spiritual strength deep down inside. Reach for it and see if it won't help you to hold on. Tap into it and watch that excess baggage melt away. Embrace it and it will carry you the distance.

I have removed some excess baggage since I started working out. My aches and pains no longer consume me. I can run that extra mile. I can achieve my goals.

I'm a working out sistah! I got more pep in my step, more glide in my slide and best of all, my soul is healthy!

Spiritual strength empowers you to endure *all* pain, and that, my sistahs, is *all good*!

Thought for the Day: You've taken care of others, but have you taken of yourself?

Tapping into That Spiritual Strength

Scripture for the Day: *Your body is the temple of the Holy Spirit. (1 Cor. 6:19)*

Tina R. Wynn-Johnson is founder and president of T&T Public Relations, Inc., a New York City-based firm specializing in entertainment press. She worships at the Bronx Christian Fellowship Church.

Spirit-2-Spirit

Is there a God-ordained spirit in the universe looking to cleave unto your spirit?

Like spirits identify like spirits. Have you identified yours?

The spirit that is charmed by the essence of your spirit.

The spirit that discovers peace with yours during the reign of "Desert Storm."

The spirit that will bring joy, filling the bubbles of each teardrop you cry.

The spirit that answers your thoughts before you utter a word.

The spirit that is free to converse, with words unrehearsed.

The spirit that ministers to your heart when it aches.

The spirit that has the faith to solely trust the other when they thought they could never trust another.

The spirit willing to give up *all,* not even knowing if they might fall.

The spirit who wills to submit, under the eyes of the Lord, to whom they commit.

The childlike spirits who find each other when playing "Hide and Seek" in the midst of the week.

The matured spirits meeting each other in the still of the night, embracing one another with the moon as their light.

Finally coming together in the natural realm only to thank God for the gift of the spirit that awaits them.

You have not found your soul mate because it's your *spirit-mate* you're seeking.

Walk into the marvelous light and meet your spirit-mate.

Tapping into That Spiritual Strength

Thought for the Day: Walk in the light.

Scripture for the Day: *Seek first the kingdom of God and His righteousness, and all these things shall be added to you. (Matt. 6:33)*

Nicole N. Brown was born and raised in Brooklyn, New York. She is an alumnus of Baruch College in New York City, where she received her bachelor's degree in corporate communications. She went on to pursue a career in communications at the Connecticut School of Broadcasting. Currently she is music director, midday announcer, and promotions coordinator at 1520 WTHE–New York's First Gospel Station.

You Are Divine

The kingdom of God is within you. (Luke 17:21)

May 26, 1996. I looked at myself in the bathroom mirror. I was fifty pounds overweight.

My outside self was a reflection of what was happening with my inside self. I needed to change the direction of my career. I was not satisfied with the state of my spiritual life. I started to cry. Then, the small still voice said, *Go to Luke 17:21.* Then, it hit me—I must take responsibility for my truth, my pain . . . my life.

First, I got back to daily prayer and meditation. I went to a weight loss doctor and he showed me the ways of proper eating and exercise. I developed a plan of action for my career.

Today in 1998, I am fifty pounds lighter. I now have a career where I can put my life's purpose in action. I now have a church home where I can experience the highest level of worship and fellowship. I am still working on me. Everything is not perfect, but life is truly divine.

On December 31, 1997—New Year's Eve—God gave me this poem.

You Are Divine

Beloved.
You are divine—right now.
At this moment—
You are divine.
Share all your gifts, your lessons and joy.

You are divine—right now and always. Mind, body, and soul.

May you always live the divine life. Create your kingdom—right now.

Thought for the Day: I am a wonderful woman of God, divinely designed!

Scripture for the Day:
Wait on the LORD;
Be of good courage,
And He shall strengthen your heart.
(Ps. 27:14)

Monique Fortuné lives in New York City. She serves as a media and marketing consultant for several not-for-profit organizations. She received her bachelor's degree in broadcast journalism from Syracuse University's S. I. Newhouse School of Public Communications. She received her master's degree in adult education and human resource development from Fordham University's Graduate School of Education. Ms. Fortuné has worked in New York City radio since 1984. She also has been an adjunct instructor at Fordham University since 1990. She has a longstanding reputation as a motivational speaker, poet, and community activist.

Reaping Joy

❧

Reflecting on the biblical motifs of sowing, reaping, and harvesting comforts me. I often revisit Psalm 126:5: "May those who sow in tears reap with shouts of joy" (NRSV).

These words speak to the anguish and joy that accompanies life's struggles. It is the realization that meaningful labor yields great rewards, which keeps me going through difficult times. My belief in God's faithfulness provides the strength to keep watering the dry ground with the hope that tender sprouts will emerge from rough terrain.

One such experience was giving birth to our daughter, Kristen. This miracle took place nearly sixteen years ago, yet I remember my joy and tears as if it were yesterday. Before I went into labor, I was confident that natural childbirth was the best option for bringing a child into the world. But when the excruciating pain of back labor became overwhelming, I asked the obstetrician for anesthesia. He informed me that it was too late to administer a pain reliever. He suggested that I reach deep into myself for strength to deliver. In that moment, God met me in a way I didn't know possible. I established a link between my will and God's strength.

As a woman wearing many hats, I often find my reserves depleted. The demands of everyday life frequently leave me feeling overwhelmed and confused. It is in these moments that I realize the urgency of tapping into spiritual strength through God's

Spirit. Just as the obstetrician prompted me to reach deep, my mother, cousin, and sister-friends remind me to do likewise. When stretched beyond my limit, I reach out to these women for prayers of intercession and words of comfort.

Often, I find myself singing the songs I learned in church as a child. Sometimes I steal a quiet moment for prayer and meditation. Problems become manageable when I tap into my spiritual strength. They become less menacing when I invite the Holy Spirit to examine them with me. The obstacles to my progress become mere weeds in my garden when I recognize God's presence in the planting process.

Thought for the Day: Reach deep for your inner reserve of strength.

Scripture for the Day: *Count it all joy when you fall into various trials. (James 1:2)*

Linda Tarry lives in New York City with her husband and two children. For over twenty years Ms. Tarry has been involved in public service. She is at once a lay minister, a mentor, an educator, a published author, a diversity consultant, a seminarian, and a member of various advisory committees and boards. A native New Yorker, Ms. Tarry holds a B.A. from Marymount Manhattan College and an M.S. in education from Fordham University. In the spring of 1999 she will receive an M.Div. from Union Theological Seminary. Her latest publication is a children's book, *King Solomon and the Queen of Sheba*.

Part 6

❧

Strength in the Storm

A Mother's Love: One Perfect Jewel

When I consider my mother (who died of breast cancer at forty-seven) and all that she was to me, I struggle to find the appropriate words.

Have you ever had someone in your life who assumed the roles of mentor, sister, supporter, teacher, and best friend, collectively and completely? If your answer is yes, then you understand my dilemma.

Losing her was more painful than I could ever imagine. However, the most beautiful thing about her dying was that I was able to reach into the pain and discover a perfect jewel: unconditional love.

The love that my mother possessed could not have been created by her goodness because she was not perfect. Therefore, I found myself searching for the power behind the person, which was the highest power—God!

I realized that not only did she leave behind memories, but she also left a legacy of love! I learned to lean on and trust the love that she left behind, and as I did I noticed that the heartbreaking "Ma, I miss you" episodes didn't come as often; and when they did, the tears weren't as debilitating. Then, as the memories returned, I would smile, take a deep breath, and persevere. I experienced another awakening as well: I have found that when I stay focused on love, I'm always at my best, and I like that.

So, every day of my life, I concentrate on the love, and His love removes the pain.

This essay is an excerpt taken from "The Circle Of Love" by Angela J. Williams. Copyright © 1995. Used by permission.

Thought for the Day: This day I will focus on love.

Scripture for the Day: *[Love] bears all things. (1 Cor. 13:7)*

Angela J. Williams was born and raised in New York City. She is a self-published author and is also a professional singer/songwriter with her family group *Meant To Be*. She has also written a series of children's picture books, a screenplay, numerous greeting cards, and a few hundred songs. Angela is the president and CEO of

Little Light Publishing Company and has recently published *The Circle of Love,* an inspirational autobiography that celebrates family ties. She lives in New York with her husband, Le'Roy, their two sons, Tyler and Tyrel, and their German shepherd, Bullet.

"Do What You Have to Do"

When a parent dies a storm hits your body, leaving an emptiness inside. At least that's how I felt when my parents died. I watched my father take his last breath after suffering many years with cancer. Three years later I found my mother dead from a heart attack and two weeks after that, my paternal grandmother passed on.

At age thirty-two I no longer had parents or grandparents and was left with a lot of emotions only time could heal. In reflection, I realized that God provides us with tools to handle many storms in our lives. "GOD is our refuge and strength,/A very present help in trouble" (Ps. 46:1).

I recall that hot August morning, feeling the chill as I walked to my mother's bedside. Yes, she was at eternal rest, but I screamed, "No! No!" Suddenly a voice whispered, "Do what you have to do." In the midst of tears, I gained strength to handle business, to begin to grieve and accept God's will.

God surrounded me with love through the support of others, gave me needed time alone, and eased the feeling of loneliness. He also showed me a vision of those I missed so dearly, assuring me that they were at peace.

We may feel a storm when our loved ones physically leave, but remember that it is a transition and we can move through it with faith, understanding, and God's love. Those we love will always be with us.

Thought for the Day: I'm so glad trouble doesn't last forever.

Strength in the Storm

Scripture for the Day: *And now abide faith, hope, love, these three; but the greatest of these is love. (1 Cor. 13:13)*

Sharon Baker-Parks is a native of the Bronx, New York, holds an M.S. degree in social work from Columbia University, and is currently employed as a school social worker for the New York City Board of Education. She is a member of Bronx Christian Fellowship Baptist Church and an active volunteer leader for the Girl Scouts in her community.

Your Will Be Done

My husband of fifteen years died of lung cancer on May 18, 1996. I was unaware when he got sick that he had just six months to live. Later, I had the feeling George had known but had not told me. I had prayed to God that he would overcome, and I believed he would. During my prayers, I asked God to heal him physically. It never occurred to me to pray for God to heal his soul and to help me accept whatever might happen.

Throughout the days and nights I cared for him, it became increasingly hard to keep my spirits high, to disguise the sadness I felt for someone so kind and loving, who had fought on the front lines in two world wars and was now unable to do anything. All that mattered was making him comfortable. I still prayed, yet it seemed God was not listening.

Night and day I prayed for George's recovery. I was so obsessed with this prayer that I failed to see God healing him in another way. On his last night on earth I slipped downstairs to pray, and for some reason, my prayer was "God let your will be done, not mine." At 6:18 A.M., my husband quietly died.

Six months later, as I struggled with my loss, my older brother died, four days after I had seen a globule of blood on my bedroom wall.

I realized at his death that God had given me strength when I thought He wasn't listening. Looking over these past years, I see that what really matters is using wisely the time God has given us. God's will *will* be done.

Thought for the Day: Let your healing begin. *You* matter to God.

Scripture for the Day: *Without faith, it is impossible to please Him. (Heb. 11:6)*

Virginia Hardesty is a member of Mariners' Temple Baptist Church, having joined under the leadership of the Reverend Dr. Suzan Johnson Cook. She is a trustee, as well as secretary of the trustee board and a cabinet member. A native North Carolinian, she was educated in North Carolina and New York, holding a master's degree in social work. Currently she resides in New York City.

Megastrength to Overcome Megagrief

Anger, sadness, and weakness were just a few of the emotions I experienced at the graveside of my best friend, Lettie. She was too young to die so senselessly. Where would the strength to go on come from? We all needed help: my family, her children, her parents, and her brothers.

"Fear thou not; for I am with thee: be not dismayed; for I am thy God: I will strengthen thee" (Isa. 41:10 KJV). For megagrief, I needed megastrength. Only God could heal this hurt.

The child I was carrying then was to be her godchild. Now they would never know one another on this side of glory. In her memory, my daughter carries her name. Her daughters are my godchildren. I never imagined this would happen. I needed God's strength to face the future.

"It's just unfair. Lettie, I'm sorry; I hate him," I repeated. It was her partner, whose own life was hanging in the balance that very moment, who had shot her and then turned the gun on himself. He died later on the day she was buried. Oh, why couldn't he just have taken his own life and left hers alone? I felt contempt and guilt.

She had lived with our family, which is how she met him. He was our neighbor. I encouraged their relationship and got her to stop seeing a former boyfriend. On the night of the shooting, her daughter had telephoned our house for help, but I had just stepped out. I felt I could have prevented her murder if I had returned in time.

Instead, I had to see her body lying on the ground with chalk drawn around it. In the background, her children stood looking out the window as all the commotion took place. We all needed strength to make it through this tragedy.

As we left the graveside and returned to our cars, I knew God had to heal my pain so that I could help others. As I prayed, God brought me to the realization that I was not the master of anyone's fate. He was in control of life and death.

Be encouraged, sisters, even during megagrief. Martha and Mary, Lazarus's sisters, surely experienced megagrief. Mary, the mother of Jesus experienced megagrief. But God turned it around for them. There are times that you too will experience megagrief, but there is a mega-God who touches in a mighty way. He will surely turn it around for you.

Thought for the Day: God is there for us, even at our deepest points of pain.

Scripture for the Day:
They cried out to the LORD in their trouble,
And He delivered them out of their distresses.
(Ps. 107:6)

Janice M. Harris attended the University of Nebraska–Omaha before marrying and moving to New York. She completed her bachelor's degree thirteen years and three children later at Wagner College. She attended the United Christian Bible College in Brooklyn, New York, upon being called into the ministry. She also graduated from New York Theological Seminary, juggling a medical technology career, ministry, and home life. Besides her three biological children, Janice is raising an adopted daughter and has raised nieces, nephews, and other children. She has served as an associate minister, an assistant pastor, an interim pastor, and now a pastor. After a move south, she helped organize the Central Light Baptist Church in Tazewell, Virginia, in 1991.

"The Grass Withers"

Death is a certainty. When a parent dies, the loss can be overwhelming and devastating causing depression, loneliness, and other long-lasting emotional consequences. My faith was tried and tested when my dad passed away eight years ago.

As my family and I stood by his bedside praying that God would spare his life, I could see him slowly slipping away. Cancer had destroyed his body, but God almighty was in control of his soul and in control of the situation. After we had remained at his side for a short period of time, the Holy Spirit revealed to me that we must all leave the room. During that time God took from my dad the soul that had belonged to Him from the beginning of time.

I didn't want to believe that my father was gone. My heart was broken and my world seemed shattered. The rest of my family was also traumatized because this was a first-time experience for all of us.

As I tried to face the reality of my dad's death, I found a source of strength and courage in a spiritual relationship with God the Father through Jesus Christ. He gave me a strength of hope by revealing 1 Peter 1:24: "The grass withereth, and the flower thereof falleth away" (KJV). This verse taught me that my dad and all humanity are as the flower and grass, which wither and die. Some seventy years ago my dad was born into this world. He grew up as a strong healthy and brilliant man, much like the grass in its season. But slowly I watched this healthy man, whom I admired, begin to fade away from cancer. I realized that his days would soon come to an end.

We are all mortal beings. But I believe God's words as recorded by the apostle Paul in 1 Corinthians 15:54: "This mortal shall have put on immortality" (KJV). Then we will have the victory over death.

Finally, may you be challenged by these words: death is a certainty. Even so, when you lose a parent it can be devastating and overwhelming. Therefore, in the midst of my storm I found strength and courage through the Word of God. Now I understand that the only permanent existence is in Christ because he gave me the willingness to overcome the death of my dad.

Also, I now understand that this earth is not my home; it is only a temporary dwelling place. Ultimately, I will have to leave it behind for a heavenly resting place.

Thought for the Day: Christ is the answer.

Scripture for the Day: *Blessed are the dead who die in the Lord. (Rev. 14:13)*

The Reverend Dorothy A. Williams is an associate minister at Glover Memorial Baptist Church in Brooklyn, New York. She holds a B.A. from the College of New Rochelle. A member of the Baptist Ministers Wives and Widows Association of Greater New York and Vicinity and the Baptist Ministers Wives Evening Conference of Greater New York and Vicinity, she is married to the Reverend Louis Williams. Together they parent two children.

Part 7

The Joy of Parenting

Empowering Our Children Spiritually into the New Millennium

My beautiful, blessed, spiritual, healthy and intelligent adult child, Tiffanie, is a gift from God. She was born and raised during very pressing times. It was the height of the crack epidemic. Fortunately, she was not personally involved with the negative side of life. She became one of the youngsters who gave advice and love to teenage friends who fell prey to this plague. Now, young women with children often ask me how I raised my daughter to reach her full potential. Usually I answer with step-by-step suggestions for raising an empowered child:

To Raise a Generation of Empowered Children You Must Develop a Lifestyle Plan:

- Every day pray, meditate, show grace, hug your kids, and say, "I love you."
- Every week attend church, Sunday school, and cultural activities.
- Train your children to do chores around the house.
- Find inspirational tutors during summer break.
- Encourage creativity.
- Don't leave your children home alone. (Latchkey kids are a thing of the past.)
- Teach your kids to earn extra money and encourage them to intern for free experience.

- Teach your children to respect elders and authority figures.
- Select spiritual professionals in your children's lives. (For example, look for a Christian pediatrician.)
- Show interest in your children's school activities; your involvement will inspire them to achieve goals and work with purpose.

Become a soldier of spiritual change in the new millennium if you truly want a blessed child. Teach your children to reinvent themselves and to look within to find their positive new attitude. Make sure they are paying attention to their environment, eating healthy, sharing, caring and giving love. You have no choice but to put on the armor of God. You must look within—and listen to your *driving, divine spirit* for the solutions. It is a life work, a strategic plan to raise your child successfully. Fill the time spent with your children with love, not anger. It's up to the parent to find self-control and to give love first!

Thought for the Day: Thank you, God. We did it together!

Scripture for the Day:
Train up a child in the way he should go,
And when he is old he will not depart from it.
(Prov. 22:6)

Roberta Roméy is a freelance writer. She is the morning show producer for "The All Star Morning Show" on New York City's WWRL radio. The show features celebrity cohosts Mary Wilson, formerly of The Supremes; Al Goodman and Billy Brown of the R&B singing group Ray, Goodman & Brown; and radio personality Chrystal Holmes. She also runs The Powerful Public

Relations Company, which represents business and entertainment clients. She is a member of several trade organizations, including Black Women in Publishing and 4 Color. She has volunteered her time to community organizations such as Black Spectrum Theatre Company and is a member of the New York Coalition of 100 Black Women. She has received several distinguished honors, including Who's Who of Women Executives, Outstanding Young Women of America, and the Hampton Music Society Service Award.

Children Are a Gift from God

As an African-American woman who believed that I might not ever have children and as one who has experienced miscarriage, ovarian surgery, and pressure and stress from relatives and peers, I value the strength that I have gained after having waited for God to give me three children.

When I was at this most stressful, troubled time in my life, it was the prayers of my husband, family, and church that sustained me while God's Word encouraged me. When a sister can't muster strength herself, it is good to have support from others.

As I trusted and waited on Him, God blessed me with my children, who have become the joy of my life, my hope, and strength. I have no doubt about my children being a gift from God. "Every good gift and every perfect gift is from above, and cometh down from the Father" (James 1:17 KJV).

I know that the words of Elizabeth in Luke 1:42 were spoken to Mary the mother of Jesus, but I feel that they apply to me also: "And she spake out with a loud voice, and said, Blessed art thou among women, and blessed is the fruit of thy womb" (KJV).

My strength comes from the knowledge that I have people to whom I can give nurture, love, and purpose and that they return the same to my life. This knowledge makes me a strong, powerful, and blessed African-American woman.

The Joy of Parenting

Thought for the Day: God, I thank you for the gifts you have given me. You've smiled on me, and I'm responding with a smile.

Scripture for the Day: *Behold, children are a heritage from the* LORD. *(Ps. 127:3)*

Catherine Tyler-Wells is the wife of the Reverend Ollie B. Wells Sr., pastor of Union Baptist Church in New York City, where she serves as a deacon. A graduate of the College of New Rochelle with a B.A. in sociology, she is a candidate for a master's degree in developmental and applied counseling at Long Island University. She is also a licensed practical nurse, a certified alcohol-substance abuse counselor, a member of the Black Alcoholism Counselors Association, and second vice president of the Baptist Minister's Wives and Minister's Widows of Greater New York and Vicinity.

Part 8

Surviving in Corporate America

Take Jesus to Work

You are my hiding place;
You will protect me from trouble
and surround me with songs of
deliverance. (*Ps. 32:7* NIV)

In corporate America there exists an invisible barrier that excludes most individuals, particularly African Americans, from management. It is called the glass ceiling. For most African Americans the glass ceiling exists between them and positions of influence, power, and wealth.

I am a Christian African-American woman with more than thirty years of management experience in a workplace that does not know Jesus Christ.

Throughout my career some of the greatest challenges to my faith have been the disappointments and indignities I have experienced in the workplace: from the disappointment of having others recognized for *my* initiatives to the indignity of having less qualified peers assume positions of greater responsibility and reward. Through it all I have survived. The secret of my success is no secret: I take Jesus Christ to work with me every day. Although I have not shattered the glass ceiling, I have attained much of the personal satisfaction and the respect associated with those who have. How is this possible? It is because many of my peers see Jesus in me.

Often when coworkers are engaging in obscene language or irreverence to God in my presence, they cease, and they often apologize. In times of personal crisis, superiors, peers, and subordinates often seek my advice and ask me to pray for them. These things happen because Jesus is the center of my joy. Through it all I have learned to trust God's guidance and to heed His Word. Yes, the glass ceiling is there, but the glory of God is above it and shines through it. Jesus has given me a recipe for survival:

S—Strength

The LORD is my strength and song,
And He has become my salvation. (Ps. 118:14)

U—Unity

. . . Unity of the faith. (Eph. 4:13)

R—Refuge

God is your refuge. (Deut. 33:27)

V—Victory

Thanks be to God, who gives us the victory through our Lord Jesus Christ. (1 Cor. 15:57)

I—Impossible

Nothing will be impossible for you. (Matt. 17:20)

V—Vain

Let us not be desirous of vain glory. (Gal. 5:26 KJV)

A—Acknowledge

In all thy ways acknowledge him, and he shall direct thy paths. (Prov. 3:6 KJV)

L—Love

Love suffers long and is kind; love does not envy; love does not parade itself, is not puffed up. (1 Cor. 13:4)

This is how I have survived for more than thirty years in the corporate world.

Thought for the Day: With God, there are no ceilings.

A Word of Encouragement to Sisters

Scripture for the Day: *I can do all things through Christ who strengthens me. (Phil. 4:13)*

Mae F. Parr-Jones is a pension benefits manager at American Federation of Musicians and Employers' Pension Fund in New York City. She resides in New York City with her husband, James T. Jones Jr. She is a member of the Bronx Christian Fellowship, serving as a deacon under the leadership of the Reverend Suzan Johnson Cook.

Help Others

And the King shall answer and say unto them, Verily I say unto you, inasmuch as ye have done it unto one of the least of these my brethren, ye have done it unto me. (Matt. 25:40 KJV)

I started with the Bell System as a high-school, part-time mailroom clerk. I remember my appraisal. My personality was friendly and I delivered on time, my supervisor told me. But under "Remarks" was the statement, "Cheryl walks too slow." I asked, "How could I possibly walk too slow and deliver on time?" The question was not answered.

From then on it was clear: corporate life is not fair.

Granted, the company paid for my education, for which I'm appreciative, and I've received promotions and awards, but could I have gone further and reached above the "glass ceiling"? Managers have said, "Cheryl you're a great worker. I won't hold you back from advancing." They felt that they were benevolent. But not stopping someone and mentoring that person are two different attitudes.

So what do you do when someone gets the promotion for which you were next in line or a special project goes to someone you must train? Do you live with quiet rage and become unapproachable? Do you stay out or slack off or become so frustrated that you're physically or mentally sick?

I found a better way to handle disappointments. *Help your community.* Do your job well, but channel unused abilities, skills, and talents into helping others. "One man's loss is another man's gain." Volunteer time in hospitals, community organizations, and especially in your church. You may not be the boss, but you can start a food pantry or a literacy program, you can read to and pray with helpless patients, or you can help your pastor realize his or her vision for the congregation.

Is my suggestion tiring and time-consuming? Yes, but the rewards are great. The Lord will provide. He will strengthen and keep you. By helping your church and community grow strong, you're edifying God's kingdom, to which we all belong.

And that's what really counts, for only what we do for Christ will last.

Thought for the Day: Today I will handle my

disappointments. I will channel my energy into my community.

Scripture for the Day: *For with God nothing will be impossible. (Luke 1:37)*

Cheryl L. Forbes is a lifelong resident of the Bronx, New York, where she serves as a trustee of the Walker Memorial Baptist Church. She is a graduate of Bernard Baruch College, The City University of New York, with a B.A. in journalism and business (1985). She is a customer project manager at AT&T and was featured in *AT&T NOW* as a community service role model (December 1996). She was a recipient of the 1997 Outstanding Achievement Award. As an aspiring entrepreneur, she designs handcrafted gift items for the "Cheryl Collection," and is the visionary behind Forbes Mustard-Seed Productions.

Finding Relationships with Other Sisters

I will praise the LORD, who counsels me;
even at night my heart instructs me.
I have set the LORD always before me.
Because he is at my right hand,
I will not be shaken. (Ps. 16:7–8 NIV)

Sometimes Christians forget how much we need God in every aspect of our daily lives. Christians must remember that the devil works in corporate America too. We must keep the Lord with us and not be shaken by racism, sexism, glass ceilings, immorality, or greed.

I prayed for and found Christian friends at work, and we are blessed to know one another. African-American and Caucasian, Baptist, Pentecostal, Catholic, and Salvationist, we are Lord lovers, sharing, caring, leaning, embracing, and praying together. We can ask for prayer or just talk to each other to confirm that our thoughts, behavior, and decisions are what Jesus would have them to be. It's a spiritual fringe benefit!

I administer a program assisting minority and women's businesses on design and construction projects for a governmental agency. A former manager asked, "How do you do this every day and not carry a chip against those who make your job difficult?"

"I am a Christian first," I said, "and I bring God to work with me every day. I get my reward from their successes and pray for them when they fail."

Surprised, he said, "I guess that helps." He didn't know how much it helped in dealing with him too!

The field I am in is steadily being dismantled. However, I am blessed with new opportunities and responsibilities in an organization that I enjoy being a part of. I pray corporate America will continue to recognize my ability and value.

Thought for the Day: Giving all thanks to God and remembering to praise him when we rise, throughout our day and prior to our resting, should be a part of our daily lives.

Scripture for the Day: *Forget not all His benefits. (Ps. 103:2)*

Lois R. McLaughlin is an usher and trustee at Mt. Calvary Baptist Church in

Albany, New York. She holds the position of minority and women's business program coordinator for architectural, engineering, and construction projects for a governmental agency.

Leap of Faith

After many years in corporate America, with several promotions and accompanying pay raises, I no longer felt challenged. The excitement wasn't there anymore, or to paraphrase the words of a song, "The thrill is gone." Periodically, I'd think about a career change, but that thought always raised a lot of questions. Where would I go? What would I do? For whom? These were crucial questions, and I just wasn't sure how to answer them.

My answer came one Saturday evening in July 1996. That evening I attended a dinner at which Les Brown spoke. That dinner changed my life. Les said two things that really hit home: "Make your move before you're ready" and "Leap and the net will appear."

As I sat listening to him I thought, *This brother is talking to me.* I believe God puts the right people and the right circumstances in your life at the right time, and that message couldn't have come at a more opportune time for me. Things were changing at my job, and I realized if I was going to make a move, now would be the ideal time to do it. But I would have to act quickly to take full advantage of the situation.

I wrote those two phrases on the back of the dinner program and thought about them the next day. Two days later, even though I still didn't know what kind of work I'd do next, I decided to leave my job and begin a new career. However, before informing my employer, I talked my decision over with my family (who were very supportive) and God. I asked God to show me what to do (and to make His answer unmistakably clear), and I told Him I didn't mean to rush Him, but I needed an answer by the following morning. Then I went to sleep. The next morning, as I had asked, God's answer was unmistakable; I went to work and told my manager I would be leaving.

Since that time, I've started my own business, doing human resources consulting and leadership training, and I've never been happier! I don't have the income I had in my corporate job, but I feel certain that will come. The important thing is I love what I do, I love the flexibility I have, and I love the challenge of being responsible for myself. I also adore my new boss!

I was comfortable in my corporate job and making more money than I ever thought I'd make; giving up that security for the unknown was scary. I realize now that financial security isn't having a job. Real financial security is having the skills and intelligence to create a product or service other people are willing to buy. While we all want to be comfortable, comfort can be limiting. Being comfortable can cause you to remain in a job or other situation long after the value is gone. It can cause you to resist trying something new, something that can bring you infinitely more pleasure than you already have.

After many life experiences, some good and some bad, I've come to realize that God really will provide for you if you ask Him. We all have everything we need to be successful and prosper, we just have to learn to recognize what we have and make full use of it (or as our elders would say, "Make the best of what you have to work with").

We also have to learn to step out in faith.

There will be, of course, some rough times, but it's been my experience when one door closes, another opens. I'm so glad I took a risk and tried something new. I wasn't so sure before, but I'm here to tell you there *is* life after corporate America, and it's great.

Thought for the Day: Be happy. Make choices that bring you joy.

Scripture for the Day: *By faith Abraham obeyed when he was called to go out to the place which he would receive as an inheritance. And he went out, not knowing where he was going. (Heb. 11:8)*

Yvonne Harris Jones is president and CEO of Yvonne Harris Jones Enterprises, a firm that specializes in human resources consulting and leadership training. She works with businesses, nonprofit organizations, and educational institutions to enhance their operations and develop the skills of their employees. Prior to founding her firm, she was managing director of employee relations at the American Stock Exchange. She earned an M.A. in human resources management at the New School for Social Research and a B.A. degree in sociology at the City College of New York.

Part 9

❧

The Joy of Aging

The Evening Stroll

Gerry lived the farthest north of the half-mile ritual stroll south on Jackson Avenue toward Muellers Ice Cream parlor. This rite of passage was part of what it meant to be one of the girls and to be "cute, calm, cool, and collected" on a summer night in Jersey City.

Jewett Avenue. Oh! There's Pat, Betty, and Margaret, right on time. "Hey, girl!"

"Ooh, I like that skirt."

"Don't tell my sister. I 'borrowed' it from her."

"Does my hair look all right? It was so

hot today. I hope I didn't sweat it back too much."

We're at Oak Street already. Now where is Barbara? She's always late. "Girl, we were just about to leave you. You got too much lipstick on."

"Oh, you're just afraid Larry's gonna look at me and won't look at you."

"Puh-leeze! He never could resist my fine legs!"

Oh, Lord, the boys are on the corner. Where are Marjorie and Delores and Clarene? There's Inez running to meet us. Let's wait for her. We should all be together when we pass those boys. Oh, Lord, I'm shaking. Be calm, be cool, just stroll on past until we get to Muellers. "I can just taste that ice cream soda."

"Yeah."

Six of us still stroll south toward our golden years. "I sure miss Pat and Betty."

"Didn't Barbara look just like she was sleeping?"

"Girl, you still look good."

Be calm, keep strolling. I'll see you at the next one.

Thought for the Day: You still look good.

Scripture for the Day: *I thank my God upon every remembrance of you. (Phil. 1:3)*

Margaret E. Hayes is former dean of the College of Development at Bergen Community College in Paramus, New Jersey. Prior to that she was director of admissions at Borough of Manhattan Community College and associate director of black studies at Jersey City State College. She has managed her own consulting firm, Margaret E. Hayes Associates, of which she was president and CEO. She has a master's degree in psychology from the New School for Social Research and a Ph.D. in counseling psychology from Columbia University. Dr. Hayes has also served as executive director of Jobs For Youth, Inc., a nonprofit agency serving underemployed youth in New York City. She has recently assumed the position of vice president of professional services at the First Occupational Center of New Jersey. She is past president and founder of the New Jersey Coalition of 100 Black Women and a member of the board of directors of the New York chapter.

To My Silver Sisters

A congested New York City subway lurches to a crunching stop. Passengers, pressured and anxious, surge toward gaping doors. High school students, gangly and gregarious, cram and jam into already stuffed cars.

Several adolescent males of African ancestry, seeing me dangling from an overhead strap, approach a seated rider and request a seat for me. The positive response is immediate. The young men doff their caps and smile. Thanking them, I tell them that I love them and ask that the Creator bless them and that the ancestors smile on their lives and work. They glow and subdue their exuberance. World-weary passengers smile. An anomaly? Not in the least. It is one of the many blessings of growing old.

I can tell handsome young men that I love them and even add a hug. I can hold babies and children on my wide, ungirdled lap and spin yarns of strength and valor as they press against my bosom. I can lend a nonjudgmental ear to their litanies and probing questions.

I can wear flaming colors and outrageous hats. I can boast of my children's and grandchild's nobility of spirit and intellectual acumen. I can whisper the sweet secrets of forty-three years of marriage.

My gray hair is groomed, my slightly wrinkled face is powdered, and my dimming eyes sparkle. The love offerings of rings, bracelets, bangles, and beads—gifts of endearment—are my daily adornment.

Spring, summer, fall, and winter—I anticipate each for its perennial loveliness.

This is the wonder of growing old. I do not regret the past as I search for the meaning of its pain; nor do I fear the future, pregnant with promise. Surely death's final call harbors no despair, for those I've loved and lost eagerly await my coming. Regardless of what the body's shell may indicate at that time, my spirit will be leaping and soaring with joy toward eternity's promise. I'll probably go shopping among the clouds searching for new colors for the rainbow as I brush the stars with moon dust.

Thought for the Day: What a blessing it is to enjoy every season of your life.

Scripture for the Day: *Her children rise up and call her blessed. (Prov. 31:28)*

Adelaide Luvenia Hines Sanford earned several college degrees before becoming principal of Public School 21 in Brooklyn, New York. She retired in 1985, after thirty-five years as an educator. Under her administration, the school earned a reputation as an outstanding inner-city school where pupil achievement, teacher morale, and special programs for gifted and talented students brought city-wide recognition. She developed the concept of a Board for the Education of People of African Ancestry and was instrumental in its development and growth. She has served on the New York State Board of Regents since 1986 and is now its chairperson of higher education and chairperson of its Committee on Low Performing Schools.

Index